# The ultimate Iceland Travel Guide 2024-2025

Everything you need to know before visiting, Top Things to do, Hidden Gems, Travel Budget and Safety Tips

**HILDA CATHY**

## Copyright

No part of this book may be reproduced written, electronic, recording, or photocopying without written permission from the publisher or

The exception would be in the case of brief quotations embodied in the critical articles or reviews and pages where permission is specifically granted by the publisher or author.

Although every precaution has been taken to verify the accuracy of the information contained herein. The author and publisher assume no responsibility for any errors or omission. No liabilities is assumed for damages that may result from the use of the information contained within.

All Right Reserved © 2024 HILDA CATHY

# CONTENT

- CONTENT _____ 2
- *Introduction* _____ 4
  - A brief overview of Iceland, its history, culture, and character. _____ 4
  - Why visit Iceland in 2024? Top 10 Reasons to visit _____ 9
- **CHAPTER ONE** _____ 19
  - Things to Know before you go to Iceland _____ 19
  - THE 15 BEST Things to Do in Iceland _____ 25
- **CHAPTER TWO** _____ 42
  - Iceland Travel Essentials _____ 42
  - Best Iceland Festivals Not to Miss in 2024 _____ 49
  - Best Seasons to Visit Iceland: A Month-by-Month Guide _____ 60
  - Essential Phrases to use in Iceland for Travelers and Tourists _____ 67
- **CHAPTER THREE** _____ 70
  - Ultimate Iceland Packing List for Women & Men (Including Winter!) _____ 70
- **CHAPTER FOUR** _____ 74
  - Getting Around in Iceland - A Guide for Getting Around in the City _____ 74
- **CHAPTER FIVE** _____ 88
  - Where To Stay in Iceland: Best Areas & Neighborhoods To Visit _____ 88
- **CHAPTER SIX** _____ 94
  - Best Luxury Hotels in Iceland _____ 94
  - Best Boutique Hotels in Iceland _____ 106
  - Best Cheap & Mid-range Hotels in Iceland _____ 118
  - Best Hostels in Iceland _____ 129
- **CHAPTER SEVEN** _____ 141
  - 11 Must Eat Places in Iceland: Where to Eat in 2024 _____ 141
  - Eat Like a Local in Iceland: Must-Try Foods _____ 154
  - The 10 Best Iceland Clubs & Bars _____ 169
- **CHAPTER EIGHT** _____ 178

- Best Iceland Beaches To Visit Right Now _____ 178
- Romantic Places In Iceland: Spots To Woo Your Partners! _____ 188
- ROMANTIC THINGS TO DO IN ICELAND _____ 198
- Traveling on a Budget - Money Saving Tips _____ 204

**CHAPTER NINE** _____ 208
- Top 10 Must-Visit Museums In Iceland _____ 208

**CHAPTER TEN** _____ 218
- 7 Days in Iceland: An Itinerary for First-Time Travelers _____ 218

# INTRODUCTION
## A BRIEF OVERVIEW OF ICELAND, ITS HISTORY, CULTURE, AND CHARACTER.

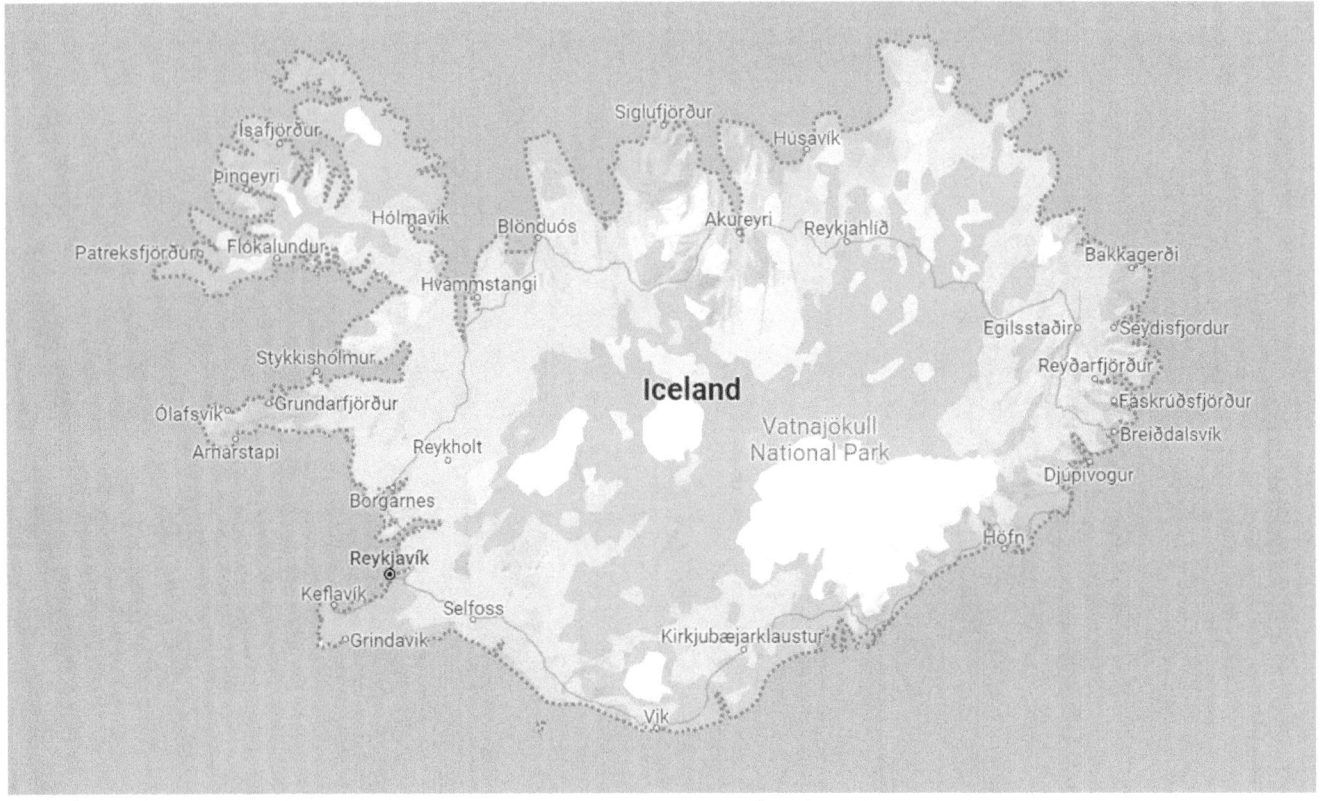

**History and Culture of Iceland:**

Bring along some cultural knowledge with your hiking boots if you're planning a vacation to Iceland. That way, you'll have a better sense of what makes this Northern wilderness so fascinating! To kick things off, here are a few of subjects. Plus, your travel companions will think you're really educated if you regurgitate these bits of Icelandic history. Are you prepared to tap into your interest in other cultures? How about we see if you can pull off that fake academic English accent?

**Geography**: In 874, a band of seamen under the command of Ingólfur Arnason arrived in Iceland from neighboring Scandinavia. Later in the 12th century, a diary documented the experiences of 400 early settlers, but very little is known about them. The Norse Viking Flóki, whose name appears in the journal, apparently failed to prepare for the maintenance of his horses since he was too busy enjoying the plentiful fishing and hunting. The first person to supposedly name the land "Iceland" was likely him. Just say it again with your charming accent, and you'll sound like a pro in no time!

Iceland is not technically a Scandinavian country, but it is often included in the group of nations called Scandinavia (which also includes Sweden, Norway, and Denmark). As an outlying territory, it is known as The Nordic Countries. Finland, Greenland, the Faroe Islands, the Åland Islands, Svalbard, and, of course, Iceland are all included in this. Imagine the United States of America when Kentucky and Virginia are merged for scale. You read it right. These two states truly include every single glacier, mountain, volcano, and breathtaking stretch of coastline. In addition to having the lowest population in Europe, it is also the youngest.

**Language:** You may already be aware that the official language of Iceland is Icelandic. The North Germanic language of Iceland is believed to have changed little since the Middle Ages, although receiving some influence from Norwegian. With a few minor differences, the Icelandic alphabet should appear familiar to you English speakers.
The next video will help you practice your pronunciations and learn some useful fundamental greetings and phrases once you've sorted out those foreign characters with the aid of this tutorial. If you're reading this and thinking, "Oh, I had no idea I needed to learn another language for this trip..." then you should definitely start packing! In addition to Danish, English is also spoken by the majority of Icelanders.

If you want to wow your friends with an interesting anecdote, you should know that the Icelandic phone book is structured according to first names alone, not last names. Why? The reason for this is because Icelandic family names are patronymic, meaning they are derived from the father's first name. Either "son" or "dóttir" (daughter) follows that name. For instance, Helga's daughter is known as Helgadóttir, while her son is called Helgason. So why not give it a shot? Can you tell me my Icelandic last name?

**Mythology and Religion:** Religion has always played a significant role in human history, and it is only one of many threads that weave together culture. Some of the most stunning views in Iceland may feature a simple but impressive church, so make sure to bring that nice camera you've been meaning to use. As one drives through the expansive, peaceful countryside, one can take in the breathtaking environment, which includes a variety of vibrantly colored flowers and even the lone church, a small black dot, perched on a hill covered in pure white winter snow.

Búðakirkja, a chapel amid a lava field on the Snaefellsnes Peninsula, is the most renowned of these painted black chapels, but it is not easy to spot. Would you want to take up the task? If the answer is true, then you may get further information and a map at this link from Atlas Obscura. Curiously, nobody has explained why those few churches are painted black; this just adds to their mystique.

It will be difficult to overlook the architectural apex of them all. The most prominent building in Reykjavik, the Hallgrímskirkja church, stands up in the sky. Knowing a little bit about those modest structures and who placed them there may certainly help you take better images, as they will undoubtedly be among your finest. Lutheranism and Christianity, which have been part of Icelandic culture since the 1500s, are what set it apart. In the midst of the Catholic dominion in Western Europe, the Icelandic Reformation was taking place, and its adherents were shifting to Lutheranism. During this time, the nation adopted a new philosophy based on Martin Luther's ideas, which led to the prohibition of Catholicism. Lutheranism is still the state religion in this country today. But in the late 1800s, lawmakers approved the Freedom of Religion Act, which allowed other faiths to flourish. Actually, spiritual and religious liberty have flourished in Iceland.

There are several alternative enclaves that have emerged around the nation, providing a place of worship for everyone, even if most of the population is still enrolled under the official religion—something that happens automatically at birth. As a result of immigration from mostly Catholic nations, the renaissance of the Catholic religion has gained some traction. But the Huldufólk's cultural beliefs are among the most fascinating in Iceland, especially in the country's more remote and rural areas. These are the invisible beings, said to reside in a realm between ours, who may be seen whenever they so want. They tend to want environmental peace in general and may take the shape of fairies or elves.

Keep your eyes peeled and your camera at the ready, since you may even come across signs in towns or along hiking paths that indicate you're in their domain! The Elf School in Reykjavik also offers classes for those who want to go even farther. Each class lasts for about four hours, with a food and tea break in the middle. This is really a once in a lifetime opportunity, regardless of your belief in elves. While you're on the road, it might even awaken your elf senses, allowing you to see things you missed the first time around.

**Food:** Icelandic mythology and magic have deep historical roots. To make sense of the country's current spiritual movements, it's necessary to learn about the cultural preservation of these figures, who are often familiar from Norse mythology. This mythical realm is home to the huldufólk as well as several goddesses and gods that stand for the elements. Therefore, the recent upsurge of neopaganism in the country should not be shocking. This is done in part as a spiritual exercise and in part as a way to get back in touch with a pagan heritage that goes back more than a thousand years.

Ásatrúarfélagið is the religion that is now gaining followers in Iceland the most rapidly, and they are currently constructing a hall in Reykjavik. Numerous legendary deities serve as inspiration for the beliefs, the most prominent of which being Thor and Freyja. All of them center on the importance of being kind to one another, the environment, and the wisdom contained in myths and legends. Anyone, even those just passing through, is welcome at the practice! Around the nation, they have weekly meals called blots, and anybody is allowed to come and join in the rituals. I can see this being perfect for mythology lovers who are interested in learning more about Icelandic mythology from an insider's point of view.

Icelandic cuisine revolves on seafood. The island nation's wealth and survival have been supported by the pristine, cool seas that surround it. Anyone who loves seafood (like me!) will discover a veritable treasure trove of unique and intriguing meals here; some of them may even make you look askance, as in a cartoon.

We'll begin with the typical fare (and you can find them in this page) that you may expect to see. One that has significant historical value but is not often included in modern diets is dried stockfish. The crispy, protein-packed snack is the end product of practically hanging fish in the salt-saturated breezes. Imagine fish jerky instead of beef jerky. Cod and haddock, which are fished fresh, are the typical ingredients for dried stockfish. In any case, it's a great memento to take home with you, regardless of your feelings about it. In grocery shops, it is often referred to as harðfiskur. Bread grain has traditionally been a costly import, therefore this is significant from a cultural perspective. This is why harðfiskur was a significant product, since it fulfilled the need for crunchiness during meals, even if it has altered somewhat due to modern agriculture.

Naturally, fresh fish is available everywhere in Iceland. Its enduring popularity extends to all meals, even morning on occasion. Having some cream cheese and locally cured salmon on rye bread isn't bad, is it? That is the "breakfast of champions" in my book, and I can think of no better location than Iceland to indulge in it. To round things up, fish stew is another common dish. The tomato or cream-based variety is called plokkfiskur. From my own experience, I can attest that this meal is well worth the price, plus it has the additional benefit of keeping you full for quite a long. You may want to save up for a small treat since humar is on the menu. This is lobster-like Icelandic langoustine. I doubt I need to convince you to give this a go if you're a lobster lover. Humar will definitely turn you become a fan if you aren't.

If you're a gourmet, you may want to look for a bread called hverabrauð. It literally means "hot spring bread," and that's right—the secret ingredient is a soak in a hot spring. In case you're now really interested, this video will show you the process step by step. As a traditional accompaniment to fish stew, pickled herring, pate, or butter are customarily placed on top of the geothermal-cooked bread.

Some long-standing practices may seem strange, or even divisive, to tourists. Minke whales, puffins, horses, and reindeer are all part of this group. You may see them on certain menus, but not all. These protein sources have great cultural significance for the Icelanders, since they, like many island countries, have been reliant on the natural resources at their disposal for survival.

**A Nightcap:** Okay, let's get to the good part! What's the traditional Icelandic method to enjoy these meals with a glass of wine? Wine and spirits were the exclusive choices for quite some time. Beer made a triumphant return in 1989. Beer had previously been outlawed. It was really against the law to sell beer in Iceland. Most people thought it promoted underage drinking.

Also, it had to be sent in from Denmark, and as Iceland was in the middle of an independence war, they opted to avoid trading alcohol and instead stick to other kinds of it. You may join the locals in celebrating the legalization of alcohol on alcohol Day in Iceland if your vacation falls on March 1st!

Open that tall, icy Viking and shout a passionate "skál" whether you're in Iceland on Beer Day or not! You have shown to your friends that you are quite intelligent, gained a far deeper understanding of Icelandic history and culture, and undoubtedly enhanced your time in Iceland.

## WHY VISIT ICELAND IN 2024? TOP 10 REASONS TO VISIT

Iceland is a must-visit destination for many reasons; however, we have narrowed it down to ten of the most compelling, the majority of which are unique to this island.

**Discover Our Awe-Inspiring Terrain:** Volcanoes and glaciers make Iceland known as the Land of Fire and Ice. These two natural forces molded the island's landscapes when it was created millions of years ago.

In my role as a guide, I often overhear guests praising the scenery for its beauty and singularity. That is just how I see the natural beauty of my lovely nation. Iceland has a wide variety of natural attractions, including geysers, black sand beaches, waterfalls, sculpted mountains, glaciers, and natural hot springs.

Hornstrandir, located in the far north of the West Fjords, is the first. It ranks high among the most inaccessible regions in Iceland. Hiking excursions across the breathtaking scenery of towering mountains and cliffs with small beaches in between are becoming more popular. The best place on Earth to escape the masses and see pristine environment, accessible only by boat, is right here.

Fjallabak Syðra, also known as the highland path south of Fjallabaksleið, is the second option. Geothermal valleys, volcanic activity, and incredibly colored mountains are the hallmarks of Fjallabak, which name means "The back of the mountains" in English. Variegated shades of green, blue, pink, red, and yellow make up the slopes' vibrant hues. This natural reserve is also marked by lava fields, rivers, and lakes. Hikers love this place. The 3- to 4-day Laugavegur Route, which begins in Landmannalaugar and ends in Þórsmörk, is the most favored hiking path. Day tours allow you to see more of Iceland's scenery in a shorter amount of time.

Last but not least is the highland resort of Kerlingarfjöll. Formerly a major skiing resort, Kerlingarfjöll is now a hikers' paradise offering off-the-beaten-path views of glaciers, hot springs, and volcanic activity.

**Unspoiled open space awaits you:**
The lack of human intervention is one of the reasons Iceland's scenery is so unspoiled and stunning. Geologically speaking, Iceland is a very young nation that is still in the process of being formed.

The most striking aspects of the scenery are raging rivers, vibrant green valleys, black sand beaches, and active volcanoes. One of Iceland's most popular tourist destinations, the highlands are a sparsely populated plateau surrounded by glaciers, which cover an estimated eleven percent of the country. Vatnajökull, the biggest glacier in Europe, is located in Iceland. It occupies almost 8% of Iceland's overall area and is three times larger than Luxembourg.

There are several readily accessible natural treasures in Iceland that have been almost unspoiled by mankind. Nearby Route 1, often known as the Ring Road, you may find a number of interesting attractions. Some of our favorites are as follows:

**Stunning Seljalandsfoss waterfall:** This can be found on Iceland's southern coast. Its prominent location just off the Ring Road makes it one of the most recognizable symbols of Iceland. This breathtaking natural attraction is one of very few spots on Earth where you may go behind a waterfall as it plunges 60 meters into a serene pool below.

The 25-meter-wide Skógafoss Waterfall, with a 60-meter plunge, is one of the most majestic and impressive waterfalls in Iceland. On days with plenty of sunshine, a waterfall of this magnitude may produce a single or double rainbow due to the amount of spray it produces. You have the option of walking down the riverbank to stand right below the waterfall, or you may climb the steps next to it to have an elevated vantage point.

If you're looking for a famous black sand beach, go no further than Reynisfjara. There is a magnificent cave made of enormous angular basalt columns, and the beach has soft, black sand with a beautiful texture. The Atlantic Ocean's raging waves crash into land with immense force. The neighboring Reynisdrangar sea stacks give the beach its one-of-a-kind charm.

Jökulsárlón Glacier Lake, situated on the southeastern border of Vatnajökull National Park in Iceland, is a natural marvel that is constantly changing. Icebergs that break off the glacier and float gracefully in the lagoon before drifting out to sea are the lagoon's most renowned attraction. The majestic mountains provide a breathtaking background. Reindeer roam freely along the coastlines, while seals swim freely between the icebergs.

Diamond Beach is only a short distance from the lagoon. Glamorous icebergs, gently melting into the Atlantic Ocean, sparkle on the dark beach. The fact that it constantly changes appearance is one of the beach's most distinctive features. New icebergs develop, old ones melt, and then new ones reform. As massive ice blocks, several of the bergs initially floated across the vast lagoon more than a thousand years ago. Many species rely on Diamond Beach as a nesting site, including the Great Skua and the Arctic Tern.

**Make the most of your time in a small country:**
Roughly 365,000 individuals call Iceland home. Most people reside in cities and towns, as is typical in many less populated nations. Of all the European nations, Iceland's population density is the lowest. About three persons per kilometer (or nine people per square mile) is the average population density of Iceland.

Even after the rest of Western Europe had been colonized, Iceland remained uninhabited for a very long time. Many Norwegian minor lords and monarchs escaped the oppression of Harald the fair-haired, the first known tyrant, and settled in Iceland. This is where the country's documented history starts.

**Get to know someone who is related to everyone else:**
All of us Icelanders may trace our family trees back to the first immigrants' voyage from Norway in 874 CE. We are all linked since, as a nation, Icelanders have only dated other Icelanders over the ages due to the island's isolation. This indicates that each and every member of the population has a common ancestor.

"The Book of Icelanders," or Íslendingabók, is our family tree database that is accessible online. Anyone in Iceland may access the online "book" at no cost, and it includes citations of all original sources.

Thus, it is simple to find out our degree of relatedness to famous Icelanders, classmates, friends, and acquaintances online.

**Listen to a special language:**

Since its settlement in the 9th century, when the majority of Icelandic speakers first arrived, the language has remained mostly unchanged. During the Middle Ages, this language was spoken not only in the Nordic countries but also in parts of Ireland, Scotland, England, the Shetland Islands, parts of France, Russia, and even Constantinople in the south. It was also spoken in the Orkney Islands, the Hebrides, and parts of Scotland.

There is little to no difference between ancient and current Icelandic, a testament to the language's resilience in the face of centuries of foreign domination. Ancient Icelandic literature, like the Icelandic Sagas, is still easily readable and understood by modern Icelanders.

Due to its complicated syntax and antiquated vocabulary, Icelandic is considered one of the world's most difficult languages to learn.

Stay calm, however! All Icelanders are proficient English speakers, and the language is taught as a second language in the country. In addition to their native Icelandic, the majority of Icelanders are fluent in many languages and would jump at the chance to put their knowledge to use.

**Come See the World's Most Peaceful Country:**
The title of world's most tranquil nation has been held by Iceland since 2008. Considerations such as health hazards, political climate, crime rates, and natural catastrophes are part of the Global Peace Safety index. The degree of militarization, the persistence of both internal and foreign wars, and the state of social safety and security are the three official classifications.

For several reasons, including its very low crime rate, Iceland ranks among the world's safest nations. This stems from our egalitarian society and closely connected culture that values family. In Iceland, there is no permanent military presence, and law enforcement officers are not required to carry weapons while on duty.

When compared to other countries, our educational system and welfare system rank among the top in terms of employment, income, and personal happiness. We all enjoy simple and equal access to excellent health care services, and with an average unemployment rate of 2.5%, Iceland has the lowest level of unemployment in Europe. Additionally, all Icelanders have equal possibilities in education.

**The first ever parliament: what you need to know:**
At Thingvellir in the year 930 CE, the Icelandic national parliament (Althingi) was established. The Althingi was the world's first parliament. In bygone days, the assembly that determined Icelandic legislation was an outdoor gathering known as the parliament. It wasn't until 1798 that the parliament left Thingvellir. Thingvellir has been recognized as a World Heritage Site by UNESCO, because to its rich history and unique geology.

**Read about the top gender equity in the world:**
Everyone has the inherent right to live in a society free from violence and oppression, and achieving true gender parity is an essential step toward that goal. I am quite pleased that, since 2009, Iceland has ranked first in the world for gender equality in reports issued by the World Economic Forum.

Women all throughout Iceland staged a nationwide strike in 1975. To show their disapproval of the gender pay disparity and the importance of women to Icelandic society, they took a break from their normal routines at home and at work.

I was a little girl of nine years old back then. As if it were yesterday, I vividly recall cradling my mother's hand during the march in downtown Reykjavík. For the sake of Icelandic women's future, I felt so encouraged and enthusiastic.

For Icelandic women, this one incident was a watershed moment. As a result, more women in Iceland joined political and government roles, and the country became a leader in the global movement for gender equality.

In all candor, I think Iceland ranks high among the best places on Earth for women. We wholeheartedly embrace the country's policy of granting women complete autonomy over their lives.

**Breathe in the colds pure water:**

Lucky for us, we can drink as much clean, cold water as we want, whenever we want, right from the faucet. Before it reaches the taps, the water in Iceland travels from the springs and filters through lava for decades.

Icelandic tap water is frequently tested and regulated to ensure good quality, unlike water in other nations. It is devoid of chlorine, calcium, and nitrate. Water from our tap is, therefore, the purest and most hygienic water available. Plus, it has the most delightful, fresh flavor. Feel free to consume an unlimited amount at no cost!

There are a lot of innovative microbreweries because to the pure water. As a whole, Iceland's brewing scene is booming. The clean Icelandic water used by about 35 brewers to make their world-famous and award-winning beer gives it a delicate but unique taste.

**Inhale the clean air here:**
Upon visiting Iceland, you will undoubtedly notice the fresh, crisp air.

It seems like there's always a little breeze in Iceland. The fact that the Atlantic Ocean contains the island of Iceland is relevant here. There are vast stretches of unbroken ocean where the wind has blown inshore. We also have some of the cleanest air you'll ever breathe, whether the wind is strong or not.

Many of us Icelanders take our pristine air for granted. Unfortunately, we long for the days of savoring a deep breath of our clear, fresh air everytime we visit.

If you want to see Iceland in all its natural glory but avoid the crowds, sign up for one of our small group excursions.

The tiny island nation of Iceland is home to breathtaking landscapes and a kind people. Experience the fresh air and crystal-clear water of the world's largest little nation.

# CHAPTER ONE
## THINGS TO KNOW BEFORE YOU GO TO ICELAND

Tourists are flocking to tiny, breathtakingly gorgeous Iceland in record numbers.

However, there are a lot of things you should know before you go to this little nation, and it wasn't always so popular with travelers. Responsible tourists will do their best to respect local customs and limit their influence on the unspoiled landscape.

Even a little misstep in these dangerous environments may put the lives of the tourist and the rescue workers attempting to save them in jeopardy. To ensure a safe and well-informed vacation, first-time tourists should use this helpful tip to avoid social shame and travel safely.

**Learn how tourism affects Iceland:** There are around 366,000 people living in Iceland. There was no necessity for large parking lots, safety signs, or armies of park rangers before the influx of tourists began to overwhelm Icelandic attractions such as the basalt beach Reynisfjara, the thundering waterfall Skógafoss, and the wild interiors at Landmannalaugar and Þórsmörk. A huge problem for Iceland has been developing an infrastructure that can handle its grateful new tourists while preserving the pristine atmosphere of one of the world's most distinctive landscapes.

**Be cautious and use common sense while you're out in nature:**

Some visitors to Iceland's breathtaking scenery have acted a little irresponsibly. A family tried to drive over Langjökull in a compact SUV, and we saw tourists walking on the Sólheimajökull glacier with shoes and lightweight clothing. One of the nicest beaches in Iceland, black-sand Djúpalónssandur, saw visitors lured into its waves, and we saw a youngster take a dare to plunge into waters as cold as 2°C (35°F) near Þingvellir National Park.

There may be no railings at the base of cliffs or ropes at the base of falling waterfalls, despite the fact that Iceland's spectacular landscape is treacherous. Icelanders have faith that people will be clever and choose not to detract from their natural beauty with ostentatious signs or barriers. Listen to the warnings and follow the obstacles.

**Make sure you wear suitable clothing and bring the necessary outdoor equipment:**
Be sure to bring accurate maps, the right equipment, and—wait for it—common sense. Get yourself a good cold-weather or trekking packing list. Think about how you would stay warm and dry in your current attire if you were cut off from a structure or an automobile. Never again will you be allowed to hike in jeans, scale glaciers without a guide, drive a subcompact vehicle across a river, or camp without a heavy-duty waterproof tent. After that, relax and take it all in; there's no need to be afraid.

The stunning Hornstrandir Nature Reserve in the Westfjords is home to Arctic foxes, breathtaking birdwatching cliffs, and pristine hiking and camping areas—all of which may be accessible with the right amount of preparation.

Fjallakofinn is one of several providers in Reykjavík offering gear for buy or rental in case you want extra equipment while in Iceland.

**Plan ahead when hitting the road or the hiking trails:**

Having a set of wheels to explore the vast Icelandic landscape at your own pace is a fantastic perk of visiting this nation. Make sure you check the Icelandic Road Administration for up-to-date information on driving hours and road conditions, as well as weather predictions, safety concerns, and, in the case of hikers, trail conditions and necessary equipment. If you want to know the ins and outs of an area, ask the locals. After that, pay attention. Create a schedule that works for you. No one wants to be stuck on a mountainside in the snow or fog without any supplies or a way to return to civilization, whether they're walking or driving.

With travel and weather alerts and information, a smartphone app (helpful in emergencies), and processes for submitting a trip plan, ICE-SAR (Icelandic Search & Rescue) runs the site Safe Travel. The Icelandic Touring Association, or Ferðafélag Íslands, is another reliable source of information. They manage several camping sites, hiking paths, and cabins.

**Do not drive off-road:** Never stray off the road. The delicate ecosystem is severely harmed, and it's against the law. When visitors with cavaliers break the rules, they create a trail that other tourists follow. Remember to stay on designated roadways, even while driving with four-wheel drive.

**Always shower with soap before taking a dip in hot springs:**
A unique gift of Iceland's volcanic terrain is the superb natural hot springs you'll discover from the town center to the fjord side. Always wash with soap before having a plunge in the hot springs. Visiting the neighborhood hotspot for a bath and some gossip is almost a national sport. You are expected to wash your hands thoroughly with soap before entering the hot springs and pools as a matter of cleanliness and politeness. Because most pools are not chemically cleaned, hygiene is crucial. Dirty jumping into the Blue Lagoon or the more distant Krossneslaug is certain way to annoy an Icelander. Please remove your shoes and place them on the shoe rack provided upon entering the changing room.

**Take a tour of the more remote or dangerous landscapes:** Experience the challenging landscapes of Iceland with the help of the country's expert tour operators. Whether you prefer an amphibious bus, snowmobile, helicopter, or super-Jeep, they've got you covered. If you're not comfortable venturing into unfamiliar or maybe hazardous terrain on your own, a tour might be a great resource.

**When driving, stick to appropriate roads:** Get to know the roads that are suitable for your car. Fingers of sealed road or gravel extend to most towns beyond Iceland's major Ring Road (Route 1) until you reach the F Roads, which are rough trails that can only be traversed by 4WD. Truly, little automobiles should not drive on F roads. Your insurance will be null and void if you drive a rented two-wheel drive vehicle on them. go out of there, or at least go on a 4WD tour in a 4WD bus or super Jeep. Likewise, crossing a river in a car without all-wheel drive or with a low ride height is an invitation to disaster.

**Travel responsibly and sustainably:** Always keep in mind the tenets of responsible tourism, such as not littering, minimizing your impact, protecting native plants and animals, and leaving no place better than you found it. This is true both in the crowded tourist areas, like the Golden Circle, and in the remote interior, where the only people around are the glaciers and the volcanoes. For environmentally conscious vacation ideas in Iceland, visit Nature.is.

**Appreciate the open-minded creativity of Icelanders:**

The people of Iceland are known for their resilience, tolerance, and lively sense of humor. They are kind, easy to talk to, and have perfect English. They will gladly share their favorite sites to visit. Being respectful of local laws and customs (and refraining from complaining about the weather or the difficulty of reaching the natural attractions) will win them over and provide you more chances to make local contacts.

Also, the Icelanders have a wide range of interests; it seems that half of the population is involved in music or crafts in some way. They enjoy themselves and are used to dreaming big. Do what they're doing and go out there.

**Take the weather seriously:** No matter where you go in Iceland, the weather may change in an instant, so be prepared to deal with bus tours and crowds of tourists. Even on a beautiful day, snow flurries are possible, and the risks are greater in the real wilds. The Icelandic Met Office provides accurate weather predictions, so you can prepare ahead of time.

**Remove your shoes indoors:** When entering a building, it is customary for Icelanders to take off their shoes. Bring indoor footwear, such as slippers or flip-flops.

**Drink the tap water:** Icelanders may give you the side eye if you request bottled water, but the tap water is delicious and clean.

## THE 15 BEST THINGS TO DO IN ICELAND

Many people think Iceland is the most picturesque nation in the world. Unmatched diversity of natural treasures may be found on such a little island. Within a short distance of one another, travelers may see volcanoes, glaciers, lava fields, black sand beaches, valleys, and mountains—sites straight out of a fairy tale.

This makes trying to organize a vacation to Iceland challenging, if not impossible. What should you include in your schedule and what should you omit? Finding time for everything on a single holiday could seem like an insurmountable task, given the sheer number of attractions.

You should think about adding any of the suggested excursions to your itinerary if you visit Iceland. In this post, we will give our ideas for locations and activities that we think are the most intriguing possibilities. This way, you can plan your vacation to Iceland with confidence and not miss anything.

**Navigate a desolate wasteland with a four-wheel drive vehicle:** An exhilarating adventure unlike any other awaits you as you explore the wild landscapes of Iceland on a buggy or ATV. Visualize the exhilaration of firmly gripping the wheel as you navigate across rough beaches and black sand deserts, the sound of the engine blending with the roaring wind. As you navigate the bumpy terrain, taking in the breathtaking, unspoiled beauty of Iceland all around you, the emotion is a mix of thrill and wonder.

The abandoned DC3 aircraft crash, a stunningly gorgeous location that has featured in several music videos, including Justin Bieber's, is a fascinating stop on certain tours. Against the austere Icelandic scenery, this haunting artifact lends an air of mystery to your journey.

Most importantly, these trips are run in a way that doesn't harm Iceland's fragile ecosystems. They only happen in designated riding zones, protecting the landscape's natural beauty and integrity. Experience the wild side of Iceland in an eco-friendly way on one of these trips that strikes the ideal mix between adventure and care for environment.

**Descend down into a dormant volcano:** The only volcano on our planet that allows visitors to enter the magma chamber is Thrihnukagigur. Does it sound familiar to you? Why not give it a try? An enormous, multi-hued magma cavern awaits your exploration 120 meters (393 feet) below earth at this jaw-dropping attraction.

Nearly four thousand years have passed since Thrihnukagigur's last eruption. As a geological marvel, the interior is still a major draw today. There is plenty of room within the magma chamber to accommodate the Statue of Liberty. This is a must-see for more than just its size, however. A kaleidoscope of spectacular forms and colors fills the room. Look about you, and you'll see something remarkable.

The descent of 120 meters (393 feet) is thrilling in and of itself, but the wonderful sensation of exploring the lava chamber makes this excursion really unforgettable.
In the summer, you should do this.

**Bathe in a tub of geothermal beer in North Iceland:** Learn about the first geothermal Beer Spa in Iceland, a place where nature and relaxation come together. Enjoy a relaxing soak in a warm beer bath made with geothermal water, yeast, hops, salt, and young beer. A beer yeast pill is used in this one-of-a-kind spa treatment to revitalize your skin and general well-being.

The low pH of the developing beer has additional advantages for your hair and skin, so setting the bath temperature to 37–39°C isn't simply for pampering. Anyone may enjoy a bath in a Kambala wood tub, whether they're bathing alone or with a friend. Even though you can't drink the water from the shower, anyone over the age of 20 may relax with a beer draught in the tub. A parent or guardian must accompany any child under the age of 16.

If you're looking for a unique Icelandic experience, try a beer bath while sipping a cool beer. Anytime of Year Is Ideal for This

**Go snorkelling or diving between the tectonic plates in the Silfra Fissure:** While scuba diving and snorkeling are popular pastimes all around the globe, nowhere else on the planet can you perform them in the space between two tectonic plates as in Iceland. The Silfra Fissure contains fresh water and is a naturally occurring gap between the Eurasian and North American continents.

Silfra Fissure is so stunning that divers from all over the globe go to Iceland just to dive it. Silfra is unlike any other place on Earth due to its unique positioning between two continental plates; also, its fresh water is the cleanest and the visibility underwater is the best. It's no surprise that diving to Silfra is a goal for many scuba divers.

The accessibility to Silfra is another great thing about it. To appreciate Silfra, you don't have to go on an adventure or explore underwater caves. In order to participate in a diving or snorkeling excursion, all you need to be healthy, adventurous, and able to swim is to make an appointment. After that, you'll be able to feel the extraordinary feeling of being in the tectonic plate gap firsthand.
Anytime of Year Is Ideal for This

**Go for a swim in the Atlantic Ocean:**

Swimming in the frigid North Atlantic may not seem very enticing, but more and more people are taking up the sport. The Icelandic people still swim in these waters today, just as they did hundreds of years ago.

Swimming in the North Atlantic is said to be beneficial for the immune system in addition to being an exhilarating activity. The water's temperature ranges from 32 degrees Fahrenheit in the winter to 12 to 15 degrees Celsius in the summer.

A lot of people go swimming in the North Atlantic at Nautholsvik Geothermal Beach. In addition to a beautiful view and golden sand beach, this local paradise also has a steam room and a hot tub. The water in the little lagoon is heated to a comfortable 15-17°C (59-62°F) using the water from the hot tubs. However, in the winter, the temperature could drop a little. In one unforgettable day, you may swim in frigid waters while grilling your own food! Nautholsvik

Geothermal Beach has a steady stream of residents year-round, despite the fact that summertime is peak season.

Anytime of Year Is Ideal for This

**See Iceland from above from a helicopter:**

Iceland may be a tiny nation, but it certainly doesn't lack in attractions. Seeing all of these stunning places in Iceland by car may take days. From above, however, you can see all of Iceland's best kept secrets in a single, unforgettable journey.

Helicopter tours in Iceland are the best way to take in the landscape from above. If you want to see the best sights and get to places that aren't easily accessible, a helicopter tour is the way to go. Plus, you'll be able to do it from the comfort of your own seat, away from the prying eyes of the curious visitors.

Perhaps this is the best way to save time on your vacation to Iceland if you are having trouble seeing all that you would want to see. Riding a helicopter is an exhilarating experience in and of itself. Leaving the established paths behind is a breeze, allowing you to experience the country's most remote and uninhabited regions.

Anytime of Year Is Ideal for This

**Go snowmobiling on a glacier:**

Snowmobiling is one of the most thrilling things to do in Iceland. Incredible virgin ice caps dot the landscape, and a snowmobile is the perfect way to see them all at rapid speeds without getting your muscles tired.

Flying over a stunning ice cap is an unforgettable sensation that may be activated with the simple twist of a wrist. Nothing beats feeling the wind in your hair, listening to the engine rev, and taking in the breathtaking scenery.

Vatnajökull, Mýrdalsjökull, and Langjökull are the three ice tops in Iceland that snowmobilers go to the most. Many people who go snowmobiling on Langjökull also take in the sights along the Golden Circle tourist route, making it a two-for-one deal.

Anytime of Year Is Ideal for This

**Visit the filming locations for Game of Thrones:**

Iceland now offers an additional incentive for tourists who are also avid viewers of the hit HBO drama Game of Thrones. Many of the monumental moments from the TV show took place in Iceland, particularly those involving snow and ice, such north of the Wall.

Due to their proximity to the Ring Road, several shooting sites are easily accessible. Even if they aren't fans of Game of Thrones, many visitors nevertheless go to these famous locations. However, not all areas are equally accessible. In winter, some areas, such as those shot on glaciers or accessible only by F-roads, are inaccessible and need the use of a 4×4.
For your convenience, we have compiled a Google Map including all of the shooting sites for Game of Thrones.
If you want to see as many shooting locations as possible, summer is the ideal time to go since some of them are unavailable during the winter.

**Ride on horseback across a lava field:**

Among Iceland's many notable animals, the Icelandic horse stands head and shoulders above the crowd. The little stature, short legs, and robust build of this rare species have brought it widespread renown. In addition to being dependable and able to withstand the severe Icelandic environment, it is well-known for its five gaits.

The Icelandic horse is an important part of traditional Icelandic culture since it was once a means of transportation and a tool for labor. now lovely creatures are generally employed now days for recreational purposes and getting out into nature. Horseback riding in Iceland is a great way to view the country that would be inaccessible by vehicle or foot.

Riding on horseback is an option at many of the farms in Iceland. Even if you've rode horses before, you'll probably find the Icelandic horse to be more enjoyable and kinder. Feel as if you are soaring through the sky on one of these magnificent beasts as you take in the breathtaking scenery of Iceland. You must not pass up this once in a lifetime opportunity for genuine adventure.

Anytime of Year Is Ideal for This

**Explore the natural ice caves:**

Iceland is a landmass covered with glaciers. This makes it an ideal location for seeing an ice cave, a summertime phenomenon that develops in glaciers. As you embark on this one-of-a-kind journey, you'll be transported to the icy core of the glacier.

Glacial rivers are formed in the summer as the ice caps melt, and they cut ice caves into the heart of the glaciers. It is not feasible to explore these caverns during the summer since they are still full with water. However, these icy treasures may be safely explored during the winter months, when the water freezes and remains solid. The sight of the pristine blue ice as you enter a glacier cave will stay with you forever.

Typically, the months of November through March are ice cave season. However, one natural ice cave close to Katla volcano is accessible all year round, depending on the weather. Even though this naturally occurring cave doesn't have a blue inside, summertime visitors may nevertheless experience an ice cave.

While the months of November through March are ideal, you may find accessible ice caves at any time of year.

**Ride in a Super Jeep:**

Probably not monster trucks are the first things that spring to mind when you hear the word Iceland. However, super jeeps, which have enormous tires and are ideal for driving on snowy and icy roads, have been gaining popularity throughout the nation.

Some parts of the land are inaccessible in the winter with a regular automobile. Particularly in rural areas, this is the case. Exploring the Icelandic Highlands or the glaciers, two of the country's most inaccessible natural features, is a breeze in a super jeep.

Do not be alarmed if you are not confident behind the wheel of one of these massive vehicles. Day trips in super jeeps may take you to all sorts of wonderful places. Because they are well-organized and led by knowledgeable individuals, these excursions are perfect for everyone.

Anytime of Year Is Ideal for This

**Explore Ásbyrgi canyon:**

With cliffs reaching 100 m (328 ft.) above a floor that is 3.5 km (2.17 mi.) long and 1 km (0.62 mi.) broad, Ásbyrgi is a distinctive horseshoe-shaped canyon in Iceland. Eyjan, a rock formation that is 250 meters (820 feet) broad, is the canyon's prominent feature. It is home to a pond, Botnstjörn, and rich flora. This region is a photographer's paradise, thanks to its beautiful foliage, cliffs, and plateaus.

Mythology abounds around this unusually beautiful environment in Iceland, which is said to have been sculpted by devastating glacial surges from Vatnajökull. Ásbyrgi is now home to a top-notch camping spot in Iceland, which is well situated close to the Ring Road and the Dettifoss waterfall, providing an excellent starting point for adventures across the country. The Diamon Circle trip includes Ásbyrgi. Learn more about it at this link.
Anytime of Year Is Ideal for This

**Landmannalaugar mountains in all their vibrant glory:** Explore the many stunning landscapes that Iceland has to offer. But you won't find somewhere else that combines the soothing effects of hot springs with the beauty of multicolored mountains, winding lava paths, lakes with pristine water, and more.

Come to Landmannalaugar, a very remarkable location. Rhyolite is the rock that makes up the mountain tops here. As it cools, this mineral-rich lava may produce a stunning assortment of mountain peaks that stand tall and strong against the backdrop of the Icelandic sky, each one distinctive in its own way.

One of the top hiking routes in Iceland starts at Landmannalaugar, making it an ideal starting point for outdoor enthusiasts. As you make your way down the route, you'll pass through verdant valleys, mysterious ice caves, fiery volcanic deserts, hills of varying colors, and more. Summer, namely the months of June through September, is ideal for this. For the most of the year, visitors are unable to reach Landmannalaugar because to the closure of the roads leading to the site.

**Spend the night in an Icelandic church:** A little church may be found in the East Icelandic settlement of Stöðvarfjörður. Originally a church, this stunning structure is now known as Kirkjubaer. It is currently a hostel after undergoing renovations.

You won't get lost on your way home since the building stands out from the rest of the hamlet! Guests staying at this converted church have access to a kitchen, toilet, and shower, among other amenities.

Not only that, but this little lodging is one of a kind. Several sacred artifacts, including the altar, are still inside. Find a spot that is different from anywhere else in the nation and stay warm and rested there.

Any time of year is ideal for this.

**Witness the Northern Lights:**

Tourists go to the nation to see the Northern Lights, or Aurora Borealis, as they are officially called. Only during the winter months in the nations farthest north can one see this spectacular natural light show. If you've ever wanted to see the Northern Lights up close and personal, Iceland is the ideal destination.

For eight months out of the year, from late August to April, Icelanders may see the Northern Lights. Seeing the starry night sky adorned with a kaleidoscope of colors is an unforgettable experience. Witnessing these swaying filaments of emerald, violet, and blush light is an experience you won't want to miss.

Join us on an exclusive Super Jeep tour of Iceland and explore off-the-beaten-path locations that are inaccessible by conventional vehicles. This trip is perfect for seeing the Northern Lights since it gets you away from the city lights, even when you're close to Reykjavik.

September through April is When It's At Its Best

# CHAPTER TWO
## ICELAND TRAVEL ESSENTIALS

Because of its extremes in temperature, Iceland is sometimes called the "land of fire and ice." For example, glaciers may be found in close proximity to active volcanoes!

Iceland is known for its diverse landscapes and temperature, which may make packing for the trip a bit of a challenge. Imagine sulfur beds, hot springs, lava fields, geysers, waterfalls, and canyons.

**A Travel Umbrella That Is Windproof:** A high-quality travel umbrella, such as the one shown, is a must-have in Iceland due to the country's extreme wetness. It rains an average of 18 days a month. If you want to make the most of your time touring this beautiful island in the rain, staying dry is essential. While it's not raining, you can easily store this umbrella in its carrying bag since it is small, windproof, and convenient.

**Help with Jet Lag:** Relieving Jet LagThere is nothing more unpleasant than disembarking from an aircraft in an unfamiliar nation and immediately feeling fatigued. You should not feel drowsy since it will detract from your journey and the beauty of the surroundings. Take a look at these all-natural jet lag remedies formulated with chamomile and other plant substances. I find that they alleviate lethargy and exhaustion, which in turn prevents me from suffering from jet lag headaches and, thus, from wasting a lot of time on vacation. I find that using them on the way back home also helps me adjust more quickly.

**An encrypted connection via the Internet:** Iceland is one of the most often attacked countries when it comes to virtual private networks, or VPNs. A "state of uncertainty" was declared by the National Department for Civil Protection & Emergency Management in 2023 over continuing cybersecurity risks... not exactly reassuring!

Your personal information should not be left to chance. Having a reliable VPN service, such as NordVPN, is essential for every international traveler, especially as hackers develop more sophisticated methods. Your critical information, including passwords, credit card details, and more, will be safe from hackers and the dark web thanks to this extra security measure. When connecting to public Wi-Fi in places like airports, hotels, and cafés, it's crucial to employ to establish a genuine private network. Also, unlike in your own nation, you won't have any trouble watching your favorite shows and movies online while you travel. If you want to save money on plane tickets by hiding your IP address, get a virtual private network (VPN) before you go.

**Iceland Power Adapter:** Electric equipment in Iceland utilize the European-style plug, which has two circular prongs, and the country's electrical outlets need 220 volts/50Hz. Do not bring hairdryers or other high-power equipment; instead, think about the voltage of the things you want to bring. This versatile converter is perfect for charging your electronics safely; it is compatible with more than 100 countries and comes with many built-in fuse protections.

**Travel Waterproof Backpack:** Do not bring your rolling suitcase to Iceland; instead, bring an earth pak waterproof backpack. Instead of carrying around cumbersome totes, choose a waterproof travel backpack. This one from Earth Pak will keep your belongings dry while you relax, ride your bike, camp, or walk, and you won't have to worry about clumsy wheels getting you from one place to another. Plus, you may save money on airline costs because to its compact carry-on size.

**Travel Insurance for Iceland:** Our buddy sprained their ankle while hiking abroad, so we purchased Faye Travel Insurance. Luckily, she had travel insurance to cover those exorbitantly expensive medical expenditures! Just getting to the hospital may cost anywhere from $25,000 to $35,000—and that doesn't even include treatment. A lot of individuals think insurance is too expensive and don't know that their home provider doesn't cover them abroad. Getting travel insurance is as simple as getting a quotation, and it's often one of the least expensive aspects of your vacation.

As far as travel insurance companies go, Faye is at the top of the heap, and their lightning-fast payments via mobile app have been a nice surprise. In addition to paying for any lost or stolen baggage, most policies also cover medical bills, airlifts, and aircraft cancellations. Get your money's worth with Faye's innovative strategy; they'll even give you your money back if you cancel your whole vacation, no matter what!

**Travel Towel That Dries Fast:** An essential travel accessory is a quick-dry microfiber towel. Lightweight, compact, and simple to transport, a quick-dry towel is a great travel companion. Towels rented at hotels, hostels, and hot springs tend to be large, fluffy, and a pain to carry about all day, so this is a good way to save money. In the event that you forget your raincoat, it will also serve as a means of drying off. Considered feather-light, this one dries ten times quicker than cotton.

**Brita Filtered Water Bottle:** Bring a bottle of brita water instead of purchasing any at the store; Iceland boasts some of the world's cleanest and purest drinking water. Aside from drawing attention to yourself as a tourist, purchasing bottled water essentially amounts to paying for plastic-wrapped tap water. The local water could have a little sulfur odor, but don't worry—it's quite natural and won't hurt you. If the odor is bothersome, you may be certain that the filter will eliminate it.

**Necklace Pouch:** Unfortunately, pickpockets do exist in Iceland, and they tend to concentrate around popular tourist spots. I think a neck wallet would be a great idea to keep your belongings safe from theft or loss. It offers plenty of space for your passport, cash, ATM cards, and phone, and you can wear it under your clothes for a stealthy look. It will protect your belongings from water damage, and it even features RFID-blocking material to ward off electronic criminals.

**Foot and Hand Warmers:** Warmers for the hands and feet can keep your delicate digits from freezing. These foot and hand warmers are as inviting as a fire in the winter and will keep your chilly feet and hands toasty. Put them in your mittens and socks; they'll start to oxidize nearly instantly and slowly fade away after 10 hours in the heat. The fact that your feet will stay naturally insulated makes them a good alternative to more costly snow boots if you're going to be out in the cold all day.

**Cubes for Packing:** Packing cubes are a lifesaver when you're on the road. Without digging around, you'll be able to identify which "cube" contains your items, and you may transfer the smaller ones from your luggage to your daybag without removing anything.

Be advised that these packing cubes were custom-made by my wife and myself after our disappointment with the cheap ones sold on Amazon. We stand behind the quality of our packing cubes with a lifetime replacement warranty, in addition to superior YKK zippers, puncture-resistant ripstop nylon, and expert craftsmanship.

**Fleece Pants:** Whether it's raining or not, leggings made of black thermal wear are an essential piece of Icelandic clothing. Wearing these merino wool leggings beneath your outerwear on outdoor excursions is a great idea. Wearing this lightweight base layer will keep you dry and comfortable all day long since it wicks away moisture.

**Security Clearance for Travelers' Bags:** Rest assured that your valuable possessions are safe with luggage locks. These locks are both easy to use and very efficient in preventing theft. This two-pack of TSA-approved locks is crafted by an esteemed manufacturer of long-lasting travel gear. A lock is a considerate measure to take since you can't keep an eye on your baggage when you're at the airport, in busy places, or just walking about.

**Jacket with Multiple Layers:** Black layers from North Face are a lifesaver in climates where the temperature, wind speed and direction, and other weather variables are always changing. Most tourists should splurge on a sturdy coat before setting off on a trip to a place like Iceland, and this North Face jacket is perfect for that. Insulated with recycled materials and fleece, this one is a cuddly, high-quality bundle of warmth. The puffy side and the fleece side may be switched out thanks to the reversible design.

**Water-Resistant Shoe Bag:** These mesh bags are water-resistant, so I used them in Iceland when my shoes got wet from trekking through icy plateaus; they came in handy and kept all grimy-wet things separate from dry items. It's a secret item that many jet-setters haven't found yet, but they're great for keeping your dirty shoes from touching your clean clothes. Another perk is how easy it is to shake off dirt before washing.

**Discounted Tickets on Iceland Attractions:** When we want to add unforgettable tours to our vacations, we use Get Your Guide, the service we recommend to everyone. Find the top tours in your area by reading reviews and then booking with the business directly.

Given Reykjavik's popularity, we suggest a breathtaking trip to Kerid Crater in Þingvellir National Park, which is part of the Golden Circle. Seeing the mystical Northern Lights is an essential part of any Icelandic vacation, but you should also make time to unwind in the soothing thermal pools at Sky Lagoon or Blue Lagoon.

Silfra is a great place to go snorkeling or whale watching, while hikers interested in the land may explore the underground lava caverns of Leidarendi or the Sólheimajökull glacier. Here you can quickly arrange your once-in-a-lifetime vacation, whether you're into geothermal bread-making or waterfall chasing.

**Binoculars Protected from Water:** Viewing Iceland with binoculars is an awe-inspiring experience. To really appreciate the vastness of national parks like Skaftafell and the rugged peaks and craters of Kirkjufell, you'll need binoculars. Waterproof and with a field view of 1,000 yards, this set is perfect for birdwatching and wildlife spotting. While they may not be of the same high quality as a Vanguard Spirit, they are quite affordable and will undoubtedly enhance your touring experience.

**Pants for Hiking:** hiking trousers These pants were tried and true on a recent hiking trip by my wife, and let me tell you, they are just fantastic. You can transform them from trousers to shorts by zipping them up at the knee; the material is lightweight, breathable, and somewhat elastic.

We ended up going through muddy pathways, so she was glad to have sturdy hiking trousers to keep her warm. After removing the wet section below the knee, it dried immediately after.

**Lipstick-Sized Portable Charger:** Large-Scale Plateaus Eighty percent of the nation remains unpopulated, leaving vast stretches of land undeveloped. You definitely don't want to go on a mountain or lowland trek without a charger for your phone since you'll be so far from civilization. This portable charger will be your savior in times of need, whether it's for GPS or a signal to make a phone call. We now never travel without power after being stuck in remote places.

**Stylish and Comfortable Sneakers:** hikers shouldn't break the bank on high-end footwear unless they want to perform extensive trekking during their time in Iceland. Even if you're only going for a stroll in places like Kópavogur, it's smart to have a pair of lightweight walking shoes. Travel success or failure often hinges on footwear. It does rain quite a bit, so be sure your shoes can withstand that. Waterproof hiking boots are a must-have for any outdoor activity, whether for pleasure or safety concerns.

**Socks for Compression Flight:** Stockings are considered "old-school" by most young and active individuals, but there's a good reason why most flight attendants wear them. These socks provide compression. Unfortunately, individuals do die from the combination of a pressurized cabin, great altitude, and the lack of physical activity experienced for an extended period of time; blood clots are more frequent on lengthy flights. You can keep your blood pumping all throughout your body with the aid of compression flight socks, which will increase circulation to your feet and legs. Doing so will lessen the likelihood of discomfort or swelling, allowing you to touch down feeling revitalized and free of discomfort.

**Hand-Held Cosmetics Pouch:** When it comes to counter space, Icelandic restrooms are very lacking (sometimes offering just a sink). While European "water closets" are designed for efficient use, this hanging bag will allow you to take your time and savor your self-care routine. It provides a built-in shelf for your skincare and styling goods and attaches to any door or pole, saving you the trouble of unpacking them all. Staying consistent (and sane!) is much easier with this!

**Headwear for Cold Weather:** Regardless of the season, you'll be pleased you packed a hat for your Icelandic adventure. You should bring over a couple of different hats or headbands so you're not stuck wearing the same one in every single photo. Instead of bringing them with you, it could be more enjoyable to pick them up at the Icewear shop in Reykjavik when you get there! They offer a great variety, so you may choose a practical keepsake to take home with you.

**Stunning Knit Dress:** Stunning turtleneck sweater dress perfect for winter, this will accentuate any figure. An above-the-knee hem gives a touch of sexiness to an otherwise ideal winter turtleneck. You may still look gorgeous while staying warm for dinner and drinks, and the locals will be enchanted by your refined taste. According to my wife, it's really classic and always receives praises.

**Textile Gaiter:** Wool gaiters won't cut it on the frozen tundra; you'll need full-face protection. Even while a heavy scarf is cozy indoors, it won't cut it in the brisk Icelandic weather. Wool gaiters are practical and cozy; they're not as loose as scarves and keep put while you're on the go. A common criticism about Iceland is that it is too chilly. Your first objective should be to combat the wind chill, as it is the wind that makes temperatures seem far lower than they really are.

**Mask for Sleep**: Iceland's famed Midnight Sun, which provides 24 hours of daylight, is something you'll get to know if you visit between June and August. It may be somewhat challenging to go to sleep and remain asleep due to this natural occurrence. Avoid disrupting your body's natural sleep cycle and get a good night's rest by using a black-out mask before bed.

**Convenient, Carry-On Bag:** Bag to have on hand in case anything happens while shopping is this good! With its slim profile when empty, this "just in case" bag may double as a carry-on for your return journey home, making it an ideal storage option for all your future gift-buying and shopping needs.

**The Icelandic delights that may be stored in it include:** Wool jumpers, lava jewelry that is created, artisan chocolates, mineral-rich sea salt, skincare items made of silica mud from the thermal springs, sagas, Brennivín, alcohol, Viking beer, and much more. It fits nicely under your airplane seat.

# BEST ICELAND FESTIVALS NOT TO MISS IN 2024

Iceland has a lot of reputations for various things. Everything from snowy winters to long summer days, stunning scenery, waterfalls, glaciers, black sand beaches, volcanoes, and more.

Visitors from far and wide go to Iceland every year to take in the country's most famous landmarks, but that's not the only draw for this little island nation in the North Atlantic. Some of the world's most spectacular events also take place in Iceland.

The country of fire and ice has film, music, art, and cultural events every year, and they draw people from all over the world. So, what kind of celebrations are common in Iceland? What times are ideal for a visit? Are they a yearly occurrence? To learn more, keep reading.

**What Time of Year Is Ideal for Attending an Icelandic Festival?**

This is a very weather-dependent question, so the correct response will depend on the kind of event you're hoping to attend in Iceland. The weather in Iceland isn't as frigid as most people may imagine.

The Gulf Stream is responsible for the mild marine environment that this popular tourist spot enjoys. As a result, summers here are pleasant, albeit a little cool, with temperatures ranging from 50 to 55 degrees Fahrenheit.

These summer temperatures may seem lower than the rest of Europe, but with adequate clothing, they may really be rather comfortable in the absence of wind and under clear sky. This is why, along with the longer days beneath the midnight sun, most festivities that are held outside tend to be held in the summer.

Even though it snows often in Iceland's winters, the temperature seldom drops below freezing (32 degrees Fahrenheit). Indoor festivals, however, are still often held near the conclusion of the winter season.

**Is It Possible to Attend Festivals Anytime in Iceland?**
An whole year would be required if one intended to remain in Iceland in order to attend each and every event. Pretty almost every month of the year has at least one event. The Icelandic people have a strong desire to create, amuse, and maintain a sense of community, which may be seen as a side consequence of that.

**Iceland's Most Popular Festivals:**
It could seem daunting to the uninitiated to choose which Icelandic festivals are worth attending. There is a dizzying array of options, and they span a wide variety of pursuits, hobbies, and interests. This list of the thirteen best festivals in the north should give you a good idea of what to expect from the festival scene up north.

**Secret Solstice:**

Of all the Icelandic music events, Secret Solstice is among the most well-attended. The originator of the event first had the idea while out drinking with friends in downtown Reykjavík at midnight and saw the energy that came from the crowd. It was then that it hit him: this setting is ideal for a music festival.

What began as a modest but successful event—the first Secret Solstice—has grown into the jam-packed behemoth it is today. In order to provide an unforgettable experience for all attendees, the festival meticulously selects a wide variety of musical genres and performers each year.

You won't find many places where you can dance to music while standing on a lava field or seeing a band play at the base of an active volcano.
Between June 21 and 23, which is the summer solstice, is when Secret Solstice often occurs. If you want to attend this event, you better plan early since tickets sell out quickly once things are back to normal after being postponed in previous years owing to the epidemic.

**Iceland Airwaves:** Unlike Secret Solstice, another music event called Iceland Airwaves takes place at a different time of year and aims to have a different kind of ambiance. The annual Airwaves event in November features performances by up-and-coming artists from all over the world, with a focus on new music.

Icelandair and the City of Reykjavík initially supported the production of Airwaves, and the first event took place in 1999 at an airplane hangar at Reykjavík Domestic Airport.
Because it is held in the winter, Airwaves is spread out among many indoor venues in Reykjavík and is more of an immersive, multi-genre music event.

**Festival of International Film in Reykjavik (RIFF):**
Due to the country's rich cinematic heritage, Iceland now hosts an annual international film festival. Once a year, around the tail end of September, for about two weeks, the Reykjavík International Film Festival is held.

Since its inception in 2004, this privately run film festival has sought to honor and develop the medium of cinema. Throughout the duration of the festival, attendees may see films, hear creators discuss their work, and even partake in unique cinematic experiences, such as viewing a film while immersed in a geothermal bath.

Mads Mikkelsen, Shailene Woodley, Werner Herzog, and Blondie's Debbie Harry are among the notable guests that have been in the past.
At RIFF, one of Iceland's largest cultural events, you may enjoy movies and perhaps even see some famous faces.

**Reykjavik Pride Festival:** Although it may come as a surprise for a tiny nation like Iceland, the Reyjavík Pride Festival consistently ranks among the top events that the locals attend each year. Protest is where the event first started. Starting in 1993, a gathering of homosexuals and lesbians from Iceland began to demonstrate in Reykjavík, calling for an end to prejudice.

With each passing year, the march evolved into an official festival honoring diversity and inclusiveness and the many selfless people who made it all possible.

Reykjavík Pride, or 'Hinsegin Dagar' as it is known locally, has been a recognized event since the year 2000. Held annually in August, the week-long celebration draws in a large crowd of both tourists and residents. Activities for the whole family, as well as workshops, films, stand-up comedy, concerts, and more are all scheduled throughout the week.
Reykjavík Pride is often referred to as 'The largest tiny event in the world' due to its immense popularity.

**Frostbiter Horror Film Festival:** Frostbiter stands out among Icelandic film festivals as a relatively fresh and distinctive event. More than seven years have passed since the village of Akranes in western Iceland was a little bit scarier thanks to this horror-themed event.

Frostbiter is known to take use of its grassroots approach and incorporate it into many aspects of the event. Unconventional venues, such as a music school, a bowling alley, or even a derelict factory, are common for screenings.

The event Frostbiter takes place at the tail end of January, which happens to be one of the coldest months in Iceland—hence the hilarious pun in the title.

**Dark Days Music Festival:** One of Iceland's longest running music events is Dark Music Days. One unique aspect of the festival is its emphasis on presenting cutting-edge and experimental forms of modern music.
It has been around since 1980 and has grown into a major force in introducing new listeners to intriguing composers.
Late March is when Dark Music Days is held.

**Winter Lights Festival:**

The winters in Iceland are notoriously lengthy and mostly cloudy. While winter may seem like it remains too long for some, tourists may have a unique and exciting experience if they visit at this period. The Winter Lights Festival is one method that Icelanders combat the darkest and coldest times of the year; it is one of several festivities that do just that.

The City of Reykjavík hosts the Winter Lights Festival for three consecutive days in February. From 17:30 to 22:00, many buildings and landmarks across the city will be illuminated with light performances throughout the event.

A wonderful way to welcome winter is to bundle up and take a stroll around town to observe how some of the city's most iconic landmarks are transformed into something completely new as the sun goes down during Winter Lights.
Hallgrímskirkja and Harpa Concert Hall are among the country's most intriguing landmarks, and several local artists have been assigned the responsibility of illuminating them. Art exhibits, performances, and family-friendly events are also commonplace in the schedule.

**Icelandic Fringe Festival:** There is an almost infinite number of things to do and see at a fringe festival, not to mention that visiting a city during this time is a fantastic opportunity to learn about the locals and their passions. Among the many fringe festivals that take place annually, the Edinburgh Fringe is among the most well-known.

Nanna Gunnarsdóttir, an ardent Icelander, made the decision for her country to enter the fringe scene in 2018. With the help of her supportive network, she was able to establish what is now widely recognized as one of the nation's preeminent independent arts festivals.
During the Reykjavík Fringe Festival (RFF), which happens annually in mid-summer (July) and lasts for little over a week, the city hosts more than a hundred distinct performances, exhibits, lectures, and art installations.

Many artists and performers go to Iceland specifically for RFF, so it's not merely a showcase for Icelandic talent. If you're planning on attending RFF, be sure to mark your calendars for the opening party, preview night, and awards ceremony. One of the best parts of preview night is getting to witness a variety of acts in a short amount of time; artists have only two minutes to sell their performance to the enthusiastic audience.

**Danish Days:** Denmark and Iceland have a long and storied history; in fact, Denmark ruled over Iceland from around 1814 to approximately 1944. This is why you may find so many artifacts from Danish culture in Iceland today. Even though Icelanders are quite distinct, one might argue that they and the Danes are genetically related, which is why the majority of Icelandic students take Danish and English as foreign languages in school.

The little western town of Stykkishólmur has a festival honoring all things Danish. During its heyday as a Danish trading post, the inhabitants of this picturesque Snaefellsnes Peninsula settlement never spoke Icelandic on Sundays, instead speaking Danish, a clear indication of the profound Danish impact on their culture.

Over the course of a weekend in the middle of August, Danes celebrate with a plethora of events and performances suitable for people of all ages.

**LungA Arts Festival:**

A lovely hamlet nestled on a fjord in the far east of Iceland is framed by towering mountain ranges. Seyðisfjörður is not just a major eastern harbor access point, but also a town known for its distinctive art and exceptional local artists.

The LungA Arts Festival is an annual summer event that highlights the town's creative and geographical splendor via performances by local young artists. 'Listunga,' the Icelandic word for art, and 'unga,' the term for young, come together to create the name of the festival.' Over the course of its many days, the fest will include workshops, art, music, and performances that will honor the artists of tomorrow.

The Imagine Peace Tower, a lighthouse in Reykjavík Harbour, was unveiled by John Lennon's wife, the artist Yoko Ono, to commemorate his 67th birthday, which would have been on October 9th, 2007.

The Viðey island is home to the tower, which points a bright light beam straight toward the sky. An homage to the late singer and a symbol of the universality of love and peace, the Imagine Peace Tower is designed to stand as a testament to both.
You can see the light from Reykjavík, but you can also go to the island if you want to. Originally only turned on for John's birthday, it is now visible at many points during the winter.

**Reykjavik Culture Night:** In addition to being the summer season, August in Reykjavík is a significant month since it hosts two of the largest public events in the nation, Reykjavík Pride and Menningarnótt, which is translated as "Culture Night" in English.

The initial intention of Menningarnótt, which is held on the first Saturday after August 18, was to boost sales at local businesses during a month that is often quiet since people are on vacation. Since its inception in 1996, it has been enthusiastically received by the Icelanders, who continue to bring record numbers of locals to spend the day attending the festivities.

The Reykjavík Marathon kicks off the festival at the crack of dawn, and the remainder of the day is jam-packed with music, events, and markets. Extensive fireworks displays are let up across the city to cap off the activities. You should go to Menningarnótt if you want to see the locals doing what they love.

**Food and Fun Festival:** Every year in February or March, Iceland's capital hosts the Reykjavík Food and Fun Festival, a global gastronomic extravaganza. The festival's mission is to honor both local and international culinary stars by showcasing the country's exceptional chefs and cooks.

Despite being an island country, Icelanders are serious foodies, and this festival showcases the delicious, high-quality ingredients that are readily available to them.

An intriguing aspect of the Food and Fun Fest is the culinary competition that pairs international chefs with eateries in Iceland. Their mission is to use only locally grown vegetables and seafood to provide mouth-watering meals at reasonable pricing.

BEST SEASONS TO VISIT ICELAND: A MONTH-BY-MONTH GUIDE

Iceland should not be visited on a whim, but it should be on your vacation bucket list. Stunning scenery and magnificent natural treasures make this nation perfect for both short and lengthy vacations. Like its volcanic scenery, Iceland's weather is quite unpredictable. The position of the Arctic Ocean has a significant impact on the weather all year round. Think about the things you want to do and see when deciding when is the ideal time to visit Iceland. Is a family vacation to Iceland in your future? To assist you in selecting the optimal time to visit Iceland, we have analyzed the weather in detail.

**Iceland in the summer**

Did you mean to ask when I should go to Iceland? Even though certain months in Iceland might be quite hot, the ideal time to visit this breathtaking nation is really up to you. Consider the summer: picture-perfect weather, endless daylight, and the ideal season for day getaways. Festivalgoers come in droves as the weather permits a wide range of enjoyable outdoor activities. Beautiful scenery will make up for the loss of winter activities like skiing and seeing the Northern Lights. Due to the pleasant weather, summer is the most popular period to visit Iceland. The extra daylight hours provide more opportunities to go sightseeing. Take a summer vacation driving around the Ring Road if you're interested in exploring the nature. Stop at the Geysir geothermal area or the Gullfoss waterfall for a day while you explore the Golden Circle. Pingvellir National Park has plenty of green area where you may unwind after a day of seeing the Golden Circle.

**Winters in Iceland:**

In the winter, Iceland is a fantastic destination for skiers and snowboarders. In early January, the area is picture-perfect, but the heat is intense and several roads are closed, so you can't get to some of the sights. Enjoy the Northern Lights and other polar experiences despite the cold weather. Despite the long evenings and northern parallel darkness that winter brings, the journey is more than compensated for by the breathtaking winter scenery and fascinating natural occurrences. Be ready for snowstorms, slippery roads, and little daylight if you're planning a driving trip of Iceland in the winter. In addition to searching for the Northern Lights, ski resorts in northeastern Iceland offer thrilling sports like cat skiing and skiing all the way to the shore. Witness the mesmerizing blue hues of ice caves and glaciers as you gain knowledge about their genesis.

**When to go to Iceland for the activities you love:**

Excursions can be enjoyed in Iceland all year round because to the mild environment, and no matter the weather, you're sure to find something fascinating to see. Here are a few of the most popular things to do and see in Iceland, as well as when you should come so you can make the most of your excursions.

When is the best time to visit Reykjavik? Anytime of year is perfect for this vibrant city, which is always bustling with activity. The capital of Iceland is usually a good time, what with all the famous landmarks and New Year's Eve parties. When you should go to the city is totally up to you and the tours you want to do. For example, you may enjoy geothermal heated swimming pools all year round and museums like Perlan are accessible all year. While the Secret Solstice event is held in June, the best time to come is in August if you want to explore the culture. Are you interested in experiencing the joyous atmosphere of Iceland? Then you should definitely go to Reykjavik in December. Indulge in a spectacular Christmas and New Year's celebration complete with bonfire pyrotechnics.

**Best time to see the Northern Lights**

Would you want to go see the Northern Lights? Tourists go from far and wide to see the Northern Lights, which are often considered to be among the most breathtaking natural occurrences on Earth. Between the middle of September and the beginning of April is prime time to see the Aurora Borealis. Although they are more easily seen during the long evenings and darkness, spotting them is by no means certain due to their naturally occurring nature. Aurora Borealis sightings are weather and Northern Lights dependent. If the sky is dark and clear, you should be able to see the Northern Lights. Iceland is at its most beautiful in the summertime months of May through July, when you can see the midnight sun.

**Best time to go to Iceland for whale watching**

One of the best ways to spend a day in Iceland is whale watching, whether you're downtown Reykjavik or out in the countryside. Any vacation to Iceland is incomplete without seeing these docile giants. As the midnight sun or the Northern Lights light the water, see the whales as they breach the surface. Fish and krill thrive in the temperate waters that Iceland offers, thanks to its climate's combination of warm and cold currents. Because of this, it serves as a nursery for many different kinds of whales. The cold winter weather makes it almost impossible to see any animals. Observe whales as they migrate along the Icelandic coast on a whale-watching excursion between April and October.

**Best time to visit Iceland for hiking**

With its breathtaking mountains and paths, hiking in Iceland is a thrilling trip. But the weather determines whether you get to enjoy the once-in-a-lifetime opportunity. with the winter, when the roads are covered with snow, certain paths are impassable. May through September are ideal months to visit Iceland if you like hiking. Hiking Iceland's highlands and glaciers in the summer is the perfect way to take in the breathtaking scenery. Make the most of the extended daylight hours by hiking the paths and taking in the breathtaking scenery of Iceland. The highlands are still accessible for winter hikes, albeit the route may be blocked due to excessive cold. Plus, it often snows on mountain trekking paths until late April. Midway through summer is ideal for outdoor pursuits due to the verdant and verdant sceneries. Lava fields, riverbanks, and hills turn the highlands into a magical wonderland.

**When to Visit Iceland to See the Most Birds:**

You will be overwhelmed with options in Iceland if birdwatching is your passion. You may go birdwatching in Iceland at any time of year, but keep in mind that certain bird species only visit for a short period of time during their migration. The majority of Iceland's bird species are in the country between April and June, making that period ideal for birdwatching. With so many hours of sunshine, you can easily see a wide variety of birds. Rare birds are often the target of birdwatchers in Iceland. The ==best time to see a puffin is between May and August.== In the winter, you can see the uncommon Harlequin duck out at sea, and in the spring, you might see them in the Olfusa River. Whether it's winter on the south coast or the nesting season in March, Barrow's goldeneye and Gyrfalcon often make their way to Lake Myvatn.

**When would you recommend a trip to Iceland?**

Due to the wide range of weather conditions in Iceland, careful preparation is key for a memorable vacation. Learn about the top things to do and see in Iceland, as well as the weather by month, as you plan your vacation.

**January:** Even if the chilly weather could make you stay inside more often in January, the temperatures are still manageable despite the lack of sunshine. Exploring ice caves and participating in Thorrablot's mid-winter celebrations are both made possible by January's mild temperatures and very short days. You will be able to see the dancing lights of the Aurora Borealis if it is on your bucket list. Take a historical Icelandic culinary tour with natives in January to really appreciate the food of the nation. Enjoy a glass of Brennan, a local distilled drink, with some traditional hangikjot, a flavorful smoked lamb.

**February:** In February, you may enjoy an extra seven to ten hours of daylight and see more of the area's amazing landmarks since they're all open for business. For the most interesting cultural and culinary events, February is the perfect time to visit Iceland. In spite of the chilly weather, Reykjavik's Food & Fun and Winter Lights events make you feel warmer. Go skiing in Iceland if you're feeling adventurous. When the weather permits, don't miss your chance to see the Northern Lights.

**March:** Although the weather is still chilly on average, there are more daylight hours, making it an ideal month for outdoor pursuits. Precipitation, in the form of snow or rain, is still an issue, depending on your height. If you still haven't had enough winter sports, March is when you'll have to say goodbye to skiing and snowmobiling as the snow starts to melt by the end of the month. Iceland is the perfect place to experience the snow, whether you're a mountain hiker or a snowmobile enthusiast.

**April:** At the beginning of spring, in April, Iceland starts to become hot. As the days get longer, you'll have more time to enjoy outdoor pursuits like driving to the Golden Circle. For those who want their vacations uncrowded, now is the best time to go. In April, native bird species, such as the puffins and golden plovers, which are famous across the globe, return, which is a sight to see for birdwatchers. When the weather is clear in April, you can view the Northern Lights for the last time this season, albeit they may not be as bright as they are in the winter.

**May:** The end of Iceland's cold season and the beginning of lengthy periods of daylight (up to 18 hours) are both marked by May. You may enjoy famous destinations with less people and plenty of time to cram in some outdoor excursions thanks to the long days. Iceland has stunning underwater scenery, so why not try scuba diving or snorkeling? Which would you rather do: ride a horse through the countryside or climb over a glacier? For those seeking natural experiences and lava cave excursions, May is the ideal season to explore Iceland.

**June:** the month of the midnight sun! Day lengthens throughout summer, reaching 22 hours in the Northern Hemisphere. You should anticipate increased pricing and more crowds at major destinations during this peak vacation season. June is a great month to come since there is a wide variety of activities to do. June in Iceland has something for everyone, whether you're looking to soak up the culture, music, and festivals or marvel at the breathtaking scenery. Is a sleeping mask in your bag? Watching the midnight sun should be high on your list of things to do.

**July**: is the ideal month for having fun because of the beautiful weather, long days, and relaxing vibes. July may be the busiest month for tourists in Iceland, but that doesn't mean you can't find hidden jewels and bright landscapes even then. Iceland is home to some of the world's most breathtaking and peaceful hiking routes. Make sure you take some picture-perfect bokeh at the South Coast's magnificent Skogafoss waterfalls. To avoid missing out on the local schools' summer holiday, plan your trip for July in advance.

**August:** when the number of daylight hours drops to 16, summer is drawing to a close, but there is still plenty of time to see Iceland's famous monuments. August camping vacations are full of excitement, as you may explore breathtaking volcanoes and rough landscapes. Get out into the Icelandic wilderness and explore its secret hot springs and waterfalls.

**September:** we begin to see the Northern Lights more often, and the days become shorter. You can still see all the major sites, even if there are fewer sunny days. Fewer tourists due to mild weather, with several routes closed for winter by late September. If you want to see all of Iceland's highlights before winter hits, September is the month to go.

**October:** As the winter months approach, temperatures in Iceland start to dip and the leaves start to fall off. October in Iceland is a lovely month due to the brilliant fall colors and the berry-picking season. After dark, keep searching the sky for the Northern Lights. If there are no clouds, you should be able to see the dancing lights.

**November:** the first official day of winter, temperatures plunge to bone-chilling levels. Even though November has shorter days than other months, there are still plenty of exciting things to do, such as exploring hot springs and ice caves. The snow-covered landscape adds to the enchanted beauty of the surroundings. As a result of the freezing weather, ice caves regenerate, and breathtaking glaciers become accessible for exploration.

**December:** Despite the short days in December, the diversified music scene and festivals make it the ideal time to appreciate them. In the middle of December, skiers and snowmobilers may hit the slopes for the season. Embrace the New Year in a style as you discover charming Christmas villages.

**When would you recommend that someone not visit Iceland?**
June through August is not the best time to visit Iceland. Although the weather is ideal, the popular attractions are quite packed and congested at this time. Due to the huge volume of tourists, costs might be rather expensive during this time. In the dead of winter, when roads are blocked and off-the-beaten-path activities are nonexistent, Iceland is the worst place to go outdoor adventuring. The mountains and landscapes of Iceland are often covered in snow, which prevents people from venturing out into nature. The limited daylight hours make it difficult to appreciate outdoor attractions, even if you can endure the frigid weather. Travelers, no matter how daring, are confined by the darkness.

Would you want to see the magnificent landscapes of Iceland by car? Experience the breathtaking variety of Icelandic landscapes, from verdant meadows to raging lava flows, on the Iceland 360 tour. The glacial lagoons and explosive geysers are must-sees. We provide a self-guided trip that will put you in the best position to see the Aurora Borealis if you are on the lookout for the Northern Lights. Tours of ice caves and other snowy landscapes are also on the itinerary.

# ESSENTIAL PHRASES TO USE IN ICELAND FOR TRAVELERS AND TOURISTS

Having a basic grasp of the language allows you to converse more easily with people and enhances your level of comprehension when going to Iceland—or anywhere else, for that matter. Even though most Icelanders learn English at an early age, it's always a good idea to pick up a few words when you go. In order to make the most of your time in Iceland, it is essential that you be familiar with the following 12 terms and phrases in Icelandic.

\* <r> **indicates a rolled or trilled r.**

Hae/ Halló

Spoken as "Hi" or "Hah-low"

As a foundational step, here are two standard pleasantries that everyone may use: hello and goodbye. In English, you would use them in the same manner. The most typical greeting is "Hæ hæ," which is said twice.

Já/ Nei

Say it out loud: y-ow / ney

Yes, the first one, and no, the second one. Although it may seem basic, you would be amazed at the number of visitors who are unaware of this and how often it will be useful.

Góðan daginn

The pronunciation is "go-thah-n die-in."

The most popular greeting in Icelandic is likely "good day," which is the direct translation. Make an effort to use this whenever you meet someone new; doing so will demonstrate your friendliness and politeness.

Ég heiti

It is pronounced as ye-gh hey-tee.

I am the one being addressed. A polite way to meet new people is to introduce yourself. Making friends with native Icelanders is as easy as introducing yourself in their language.

Hvar eris

pronounced kva-ee-ah.

"Where is" is represented by this. It will be good to know how to ask for directions since, let's face it, no one ever knows their way around an unfamiliar place. The locals will likely understand what you mean, so knowing the Icelandic name of the site you are attempting to discover is not necessary.

Klósett

Spelled "k-low-seht"

This term refers to the restroom or the toilet. Everyone has been there, man. Being in a foreign nation does not alter the fact that you have to go when you have to go. If you know this term, you may use it to read signs or ask a local for directions to a bathroom.

Hversu mikið kostar þetta?

Vowels pronounced as kve"Choo-stah-su mih-kith" That's right.

"How much is this?" is the meaning here. Knowing how much anything costs can come in handy when buying meals or souvenirs. Keep in mind that the Icelandic word for crown is krónur. The word "kall," meaning "bucks" in English, is another possible term they may choose.

The name Kvitunn

Word pronunciation: kv-ih-tuhn

"Receipt" is what this implies. Recognizing the term will help you respond positively when asked whether you would want one. The following options, yes or no, are available for your consideration.

Þakka þér/Takk

The pronunciation is thah-kah th-yeh-<r> / tah-k.

Both express gratitude, although the first one is more formally used. "Takk" means "thanks" in our language.

Afsakið/ Fyrirgefðu

The sound is pronounced as af-sah-kith / fih- -if <r>-gef thu

"Sorry" is the same as "excuse me," however the second is more formally used.

Verði þér góður

Voiced: veh-<r>[thu th-yeh] pass through

Please feel free to use this phrase how you want. It is necessary to respond with "thank you" or anything like if someone says it in Iceland since proper behavior is highly valued. This is mentioned in point number eight.

Bless

Pronounced as bleh-s, bless

"Bye" or "goodbye" is the meaning here. Bless bless is a common phrase that is said twice, much like the greeting.

You may embark on your trips with greater confidence and comfort now that you know some of the fundamentals of the Icelandic language. Have a safe journey and good luck! The friendly staff at Berjaya Hotels would love to have you stay at one of their many comfortable properties across Iceland so that you may put your newly-acquired Icelandic skills to the test. Good day!

# CHAPTER THREE
## ULTIMATE ICELAND PACKING LIST FOR WOMEN & MEN (INCLUDING WINTER!)

When I go outside, the only thing that matters to me is that I am warm and comfortable, not how I seem. So, take it from an Icelandic resident who goes hiking every weekend: be practical with your gear!

When planning your Icelandic vacation, keep in mind the following three points: layers, comfort, and water/windproof clothing.

**Wind & Waterproof Parka:** Your Icelandic winter wardrobe isn't complete without a wind and waterproof parka.

The first time I came here, it was in the dead of winter. Along with my fur hoodie, I brought my stunning Michael Kors jacket, which is water-resistant. The significance of having waterproof gear became immediately apparent to me.

I obviously didn't know what to bring for wintertime Iceland since I was wet in less than five minutes of being outside in the rain.

Remember the sideways rain, therefore you need a warm, water-resistant jacket with a hood.

The more protected you are, the better, so anything knee-length, like this basic winter parka, is ideal!

Among the greatest coats to wear in November, when snow and rain are commonplace in Iceland, is this one.

**Pants:** Jeans are OK for lounging around the house, but they won't protect you from the elements while you're adventuring.

If your pants or leggings become wet, you're basically toast for the day. You should wear something to keep your legs warm and dry, believe me.

For outdoor snow pants lined with fleece, I have one pair that I can use on snowy outings. On days when it's raining or windy, I have a lighter pair that I like! I would definitely bring a pair of these nasty boys to Iceland if I were you, whether I were there in March or December.

**Down coat:** Photo of Jeannie Capturing Winter Scenes at Skogafoss in a Waterproof Raincoat | Iceland Winter Packing Guide | Iceland with a View

If Reykjavík is to be explored on foot during warm weather, this may serve as an excellent outer layer on its own.

But as the weather becomes cooler, this coat will serve as a cozy undergarment. Down is an excellent insulator, plus it's lightweight, compact, and easy to transport.

I really love this Wantdo jacket. It contains duck down that has been approved by the Responsible Down Standard (RDS) and is sourced in an ethical manner.

**Hat / Headband:** Regardless of the season, I almost always wear a hat. In Iceland, you should absolutely wear warm clothing, especially for your head and ears.

I always wear my headband, although on very cold days I go for a longer one.

Love Your Melon makes the most lovely ones, and my favorite sort has a snug weave for optimum warmth.

**Gloves:** Mittens aren't practical for me since I'm always taking pictures, thus gloves are a better choice.
In addition to being a terrific alternative, these touchscreen gloves from Tomily are also windproof.
Thanks to the touchscreen pads, you won't even need to remove your gloves to use your phone!
I would recommend include it in your winter Iceland packing list because to how handy it is.

**Woven scarf:** I am quite concerned about keeping my neck warm. My wool scarf is fantastic at keeping the wind at bay.
I use these merino wool gaiters often since a scarf may be cumbersome. I like that they are double-layered and do not cause any itching. For days when it's chilly outside or while adventuring, I also have a gaiter lined with fleece.

**Layers:** The key to surviving the cold Icelandic winters is to wear many layers of clothing. That way, you may simply modify your wardrobe to adapt to the unpredictable weather.

**Thermals:** My go-to thermal is Under Armour because it keeps me warm and dries fast. A high-quality foundation layer will do wonders for your thermal efficiency, so don't compromise on this area. Always have a top and a bottom on hand; you can wear them under anything.

**Fleece leggings:** Wearing them on their own or beneath hiking pants is another viable alternative. Even though it's not often, I can sometimes get away with my fleece leggings alone, sans my outside trousers.

**Wool sweater:** Get a wool sweater; it's a no-brainer! This is very revolutionary. Hold off till you get here if you'd rather get an authentic Icelandic Lopapeysa. Not only are they very cozy, but they also serve a practical purpose by naturally repelling water. I wear mine every weekend; it's the coziest thing I possess. Trust me when I say that!

**Wool socks:** Several pairs of wool socks that can wick away moisture are a must. For cooler days, I would bring wool socks in addition to my standard hiking socks. Am I showing my passion for wool? When it comes to staying warm, nothing compares!

**Layering long-sleeves:** The perfect winter layering piece is a long-sleeved shirt, dry-fit zip-up, toasty cardigan, or that charming chambray button-up. You can switch up your dinner attire with these items, so you won't have to wear the same thing every day.

**Jeans:** Remember that comfort is paramount, thus jeans are not the way to go for your outdoor pursuits. Going out to eat, nevertheless, calls for jeans. Skinny jeans are popular in Iceland.

Staying dry and warm should be your first priority when it comes to winter apparel. It's better to be prepared than sorry!

# CHAPTER FOUR
## GETTING AROUND IN ICELAND - A GUIDE FOR GETTING AROUND IN THE CITY

Those with an adventurous spirit are invited to Iceland, the country of fire and ice, to discover its secret nooks and marvel at its magnificent wildlife. There are a variety of transportation options in this stunning nation, each with its own advantages and disadvantages, so planning your trip around it is essential.

Getting about Iceland is like embarking on a magical journey; the trick to discovering everything it has to offer is all in how you get around. Renting a vehicle, taking a bus, hailing a cab, going on a tour, or even flying across continents are all viable choices to consider when planning your trip, depending on your interests, money, and schedule.

Your vacation tastes, budget, and desired degree of exploration will determine the optimal form of transportation. A vehicle rental is the way to go if you want to see off-the-beaten-path attractions and satisfy your need for freedom. If you want to discover all the secret corners, combine this with ferries.

Tours and buses are convenient for guided activities and smooth transfers. While aircraft are necessary for effectively traveling big distances, taxis are suitable for short travels inside cities. Before deciding on a mode of transportation to see Iceland, think about your schedule and what's most important to you.

**Rental Car Services in Iceland:**
Many vacationers choose to hire a vehicle so they may have the most freedom and flexibility. Driving throughout Iceland is a great way to see the country at your own speed, away from the crowds, and maybe even encounter some wild, unspoiled landscapes.

Ring Road makes it easy to reach many of the island's attractions, while F-roads go to more rural and untamed areas. Indulge in the sensation of driving across a variety of scenery, from volcanic vistas to waterfalls.

**The Benefits and Drawbacks of Renting a Car in Iceland:**

The definition of independence and adventure is driving throughout Iceland in a rented automobile. When you have a car, you can go where you want, when you want, and find all the best spots. There is no better way to see the Northern Lights than at your own pace while stopping at any vantage point and venturing into secluded regions.

But, renting a vehicle isn't without its difficulties, especially for those who aren't used to driving in bad weather or who are traveling alone. Icelandic weather and road conditions are notoriously difficult to anticipate, particularly in the winter. To rent a vehicle securely in the winter, you actually need to have experience driving in winter conditions and a trip companion. Furthermore, it is highly recommended to reserve your rental vehicle in advance to avoid paying a fortune.

**Icelandic car rentals:**

The price of renting a car in Iceland might change based on factors including the season, the length of the rental, and the specific model you choose. Prices tend to be higher during the summer, when there are a lot of tourists. While 4×4 vehicles are essential for off-road activities and F-roads, compact automobiles tend to be more budget-friendly.

**The Icelandic Fuel Market:**

It is worth filling up at every fuel station you come across in Iceland, particularly in the more rural locations, since gas stations are not common everywhere. On the major highways throughout the nation, you won't have to worry about gas stations, but in the outlying areas of the Highlands and Westfjords, you could.

Although some gas stations in Iceland do have employees, most are self-service and accept credit cards. A hold that is placed on your card when you pay for gas is often withdrawn within a few days, so there's no need to be worried.

**Icelandic Parking:**

Parking is seldom a problem in Iceland due to the country's large open areas and relatively low automobile density. Large parking lots are available at most sites, and some even provide parking meters or online payment options. As most people in Iceland have access to the internet, Parka.is has become the most popular parking app in the country.

Finding a parking spot in Reykjavík can be trickier. There are a few free spots near Hallsgrímskirkja and the National Museum of Iceland, but most parking is charged. You can find parking on other streets, but you'll have to pay for the privilege. An hourly rate of 200ISK (about £1.20) to 385ISK (about £2.30) is available.

Always Park facing the direction of traffic flow while parking on the street; otherwise, you may be subject to a fine. You should double-check that the parking lot you're in is not private.

**Iceland's Toll Roads:**

In all of Iceland, only one route requires a toll. In 2020, just outside of Akureyri in north Iceland, the Vaðlaheiðargöng tunnel was inaugurated. The 16-kilometer route along Ring Road Route 1 may be shortened thanks to the tunnel that links Akureyri to the east bank of the Eyjafjörður fjord.

Each journey through the tunnel costs 1,500ISK (£8.85) for a regular automobile and 2,500ISK (£14.75) for a bigger vehicle. All payments must be made online and made no later than 24 hours before to or after the tunnel is used. A single tip may be purchased on the veggjald.is website at this link.
To circumvent the toll, one may use Route 83 and Route 84 via Svalbarðseyri and travel around the peninsula. The trip is longer, but it goes through some stunning scenery.

**Things to Think About When Hiring an Icelandic Car Rental:**
- Get the best deals and guaranteed availability by booking ahead of time.
- Pick a car that works for your schedule and the weather.
- Read up on the laws and conditions of the Icelandic roads.
- Get peace of mind by purchasing comprehensive insurance.
- To account for any weather or photo stoppage delays, include additional time to your schedule.

**Icelandic Bus Tours:**

Those who would prefer not to have as much responsibility behind the wheel can consider taking the bus. The Icelandic bus system provides regular routes with knowledgeable drivers to most of the country's main cities and tourist hotspots. Traveling by bus or train is a great way to see the sights and meet new people, but it doesn't have the same level of spontaneity as driving oneself.

Taking the bus to Þórsmörk and Landmannalaugar instead of a full tour or trying to drive yourself is a fantastic option for anybody wishing to see the Highlands.

**Traveling by bus in Iceland: the pros and cons**

If you'd rather not deal with traffic or other driving-related issues, taking a bus in Iceland is a great option. Additionally, it's a great opportunity to meet other travelers.

But, because you'll have to stick to set routes and schedules, using a bus can make you less spontaneous. Standard bus lines don't often reach outlying places, therefore it may not be the best option for touring such areas.

When traveling inside Reykjavík and Akureyri, using a bus is a great way to get about Iceland, however schedules might be lacking outside of the cities. Make careful to factor in bus timings when planning your trip if you want to use the bus.

**What Does It Cost to Travel by Bus in Iceland?**

Icelandic bus travel is reasonably priced, and there are a variety of ticket choices to suit different routes and durations. For longer trips, it might be more economical to purchase a multi-day ticket or a tourist card. Taking the Hop-on-Hop-off bus is a great way to visit Reykjavík's sites.

Price of a single Reykjavik bus ticket: 470 ISK (about £2.80).

Bus 940ISK (£5.60) runs at night.

Passengers with disabilities, elderly individuals (over 67 years old), and youths (aged 6–17) 235ISK (£1.40).

There is no cost for children under the age of 6.

**Some Things to Think About Before Using the Bus in Iceland:**

Do your homework and plan out your routes ahead of time.

Make sure you get to the bus stations on time by checking the schedules.

Get more bang for your buck by snagging a flexible pass or one that covers several days.

Take use of Straetó's website and app to buy tickets and map out your travels.

**Icelandic Taxes:**

In cities and towns, taxis are easily accessible and perfect for shorter journeys inside the city or town. While they may be pricey for long-distance travel, they can come in handy in bad weather or when you need to go somewhere fast.

**Does Iceland have a Bolt or Uber?**

Iceland does not have an Uber or Bolt. Get in touch with your host or the front desk at your hotel if you need a cab. Taxis are few outside of Akureyri and Reykjavík.

**Taxis in Iceland: the pros and the cons**

Taking a taxi in Reykjavik or any other major city in Iceland is quick, easy, and cheap. For shorter journeys or in areas with limited public transit options, their door-to-door service is perfect.

Taxis, on the other hand, may be pricey, particularly when going a long way or to a faraway place. During popular tourist times, it would be wise to make a reservation in advance to secure a spot. You may want to consider auto rental as an alternative to taxis in more isolated places if you want to really escape the crowds.

**How Much Do Taxes Cost in Iceland?**

Taxis in Iceland operate on a metered basis, and depending on the time of day, you may pay more or less depending on the day of the week. Keep in mind that extra charges could be incurred for things like extra luggage or specific requests.

Like other services in the nation, taxis in Iceland charge exorbitant rates. An example of a taxi fare is shown below:

Price: 730ISK (£4.30) lowest fare

Two pounds, or 341 ISK, per kilometer

It costs 7,920 ISK (£46.71) for an hour of waiting.

**Road Taxi from Reykjavík to Keflavík Airport:**

The route connecting Reykjavik's central business district and Keflavik Airport is among the most often travelled by taxi in Iceland. This journey's pricing is subject to change based on traffic conditions. The average time is 45 minutes, and the price range is 16,000ISK (£95–20,000ISK, or £120–120).

Taking the FlyBus to the airport and spending the night in Keflavík would be a more convenient option if you're seeking a cheaper cab cost. From Keflavík to the airport, the cost of a cab is around 2,000ISK, or £12.

**What to keep in mind when hoping into an ice taxi:**

To be sure you're getting a fair price and a safe ride, choose an approved taxi service.
Get a quote for the fare before you go off.
Think about taking a group cab or using a rideshare service to split the cost.

**Icelandic Tours:**

To really immerse yourself and get profound insights, guided excursions are the way to go. By signing up for a tour, you can relax and enjoy yourself while the professionals take care of the details. Adventurers with varying interests and schedules may choose from a wide variety of programs, including exciting hikes on glaciers, tours of the Northern Lights, and wildlife excursions.

**The benefits and disadvantages of visiting iceland:**

Icelandic tours provide customized experiences, knowledgeable guides, and easy logistics. Travel with knowledgeable experts who can fill you in on the intriguing history, geology, and culture of the places you visit.

But guided tours may have predetermined schedules, so there's less room for creativity. During the busiest times of year, even the most popular trips might seem overcrowded.

**Vacation Packages to Iceland:**

The time, kind of activity, and contents of a tour determine its price. Some trips may seem pricey, but they usually include transportation, expert guides, and equipment.
Important Considerations for an Icelandic Vacation
Do your homework and choose trustworthy tour companies.
To guarantee top-notch encounters, read reviews and look at ratings.
Take into account your hobbies and degree of physical health while choosing a trip.

**Icelandic Air Travel:**

View of Iceland's snowy landscape from above

**Icelandic Flights:**

Domestic flights are perfect for getting to remote parts of Iceland when time is of the essence or when seeing the whole country is out of the question. They link large cities to outlying regions, allowing people to save time and reach places that might otherwise be unreachable.

There is a tiny airport in every part of Iceland, and during the winter when highways are blocked, these airports may become a lifeline. In the event of inclement weather, flights may be canceled. Rest assured; Iceland Air will promptly reschedule your journey whenever the weather improves.

**Details regarding flights to Iceland:**
Taking a domestic flight in Iceland is a quick and easy option to travel long distances. You can't go to isolated locations that aren't accessible by road, and they also provide a breathtaking perspective of Iceland's breathtaking scenery.

Flying, on the other hand, could not afford you the same opportunities to see the scenery at ground level as other forms of transportation. Compared to buses or rental cars, it's also more expensive.

Arriving at a small airport also requires you to consider transportation options. Because of the scarcity of buses and the high cost of taxis, renting a vehicle may be your only viable alternative.

**How Much Do Flights to Iceland Cost?**
Distance, time of year, and airline all have a role in determining the price of a domestic trip. Save money on your flight by planning ahead and being flexible with your departure and arrival dates.

**What to keep in mind before your flight to Iceland:**
Think about how ground exploration and time savings compare.
Before you book, make sure you know the baggage limitations and any extra costs.
To get the best deals and availability, book your flight in advance.

**Icelandic Ferry Travel:**

One of the most interesting and picturesque ways to see Iceland's beautiful coastline and neighboring islands is via ferry. Ferries may not cover as much ground as other forms of transportation, but they provide a beautiful way to see the Icelandic landscape from the water.

On a road trip throughout Iceland, the two most typical ferry rides are to the Westman Islands (from Landeyjahöfn to Vestmannaeyjar) and the Bladur ferry (from Brjánslækur to Stykkishólmur) across Breiðafjörður.

**The Benefits and Drawbacks of Taking a Ferry in Iceland:**
You may get a new viewpoint on Iceland's untamed shores, magnificent fjords, and beautiful islands by hopping on a boat. Traveling at a slower pace gives you more time to take in the stunning scenery and, who knows, maybe even see some marine life.

The availability of services may also vary by season, and there may be restrictions on the routes that ferries may take. Furthermore, using a boat may not be the most effective use of your time if you are running behind schedule, particularly if you have a large distance to go.

**How Much Does a Ferry Ride Across Iceland Cost?**
Route, length, and cabin selection determine the price of an Icelandic ferry ticket. Longer voyages along the coast may be somewhat expensive, while shorter cruises between adjacent islands are usually more reasonable.

**Things to Think About Before Taking an Icelandic Ferry:**
Particularly on less-traveled routes, it is advisable to check the boat schedule and availability ahead of time.
Be sure to pack warm clothing since the weather on the cruise might change unexpectedly.
If you want to be sure you're comfortable on longer trips, consider hiring a cabin.

**Icelandic Accessibility:** We strive to make Iceland an accessible and welcoming place for all types of travelers, including those with impairments. Numerous landmarks, hotels, and transportation providers have made efforts to accommodate all tourists.

**When you plan your trip around Iceland, be sure to:**
It is an experience of a lifetime to discover the secret nooks and animals of Iceland. Picking the correct kind of transportation allows you to tailor an experience to your tastes and objectives. Whether you choose the independence of a rental vehicle, the ease of a guided tour, or the excitement of a bus, the breathtaking scenery of Iceland will make a lasting impression on your soul. In Iceland, where nature is king, you may experience a wide variety of landscapes, meet rare animals, and lose yourself in its mesmerizing allure.

- The flexibility of a rented car comes with the downsides of being subject to the elements and budget constraints.
- Traveling by bus offers guided tours and is a budget-friendly option.
- Although they are handy, taxis may be pricey when traveling large distances.
- On tours, you'll have the benefit of knowledgeable guides and well-planned experiences.
- While flying allows for fast long-distance travel, there is little room for exploring while on land.
- Because of this, you should prepare ahead of time to ensure that your ferry schedule fits your needs.

- Accessibility for people with impairments is a priority for Iceland.

Is an Icelandic Road trip in your future? Glance over all of my Iceland Travel Guides

# CHAPTER FIVE
## WHERE TO STAY IN ICELAND: BEST AREAS & NEIGHBORHOODS TO VISIT

If you're searching for the top Icelandic hotels, you could just stumble onto your dream vacation spot. Whether you're in the middle of nowhere or in the middle of nowhere in the nation, you'll never be far from a breathtaking natural feature, whether it's a mighty waterfall, a picturesque fishing town, or some delicious cuisine.

**Accommodations in Iceland:**

Depending on your preferences, deciding where to stay in Iceland might be somewhat more challenging. Are they the Northern Lights? Urban living? Spectacular scenery? Have no fear; we are here to help when the options seem too many.

**Reykjavík the capital of Iceland for cultural cool:**

The capital of Iceland, Reykjavík, is known for its cultural coolness.

Even though it is situated in the middle of nowhere in the Atlantic Ocean, Reykjavík is just as trendy as any other city in the globe. Decorated with vibrant street art, it has delectable eateries, charming cafés, and brightly colored buildings. Read our recommendations for the top eateries in Reykjavik.

You must make an effort to spend some time here if you want to experience the wonderful Icelandic culture that we have grown to appreciate on an international level. The city is one of the top spots to visit in Iceland this summer, and it also happens to be one of the 30 greatest locations to take kids. It's a fantastic starting point for any kind of vacationer.

**Where to stay in Reykjavik:**

**For budget stays:** You won't find a more basic accommodation than Kex accommodation. It has a cafe-bar, live performances, a gym, and is hip, fashionable, and quirky; guests may choose between dormitories and private rooms.

**For luxury stays:** Staying at the Radisson Blu 1919, a five-star hotel, will put you within ten minutes of Reykjavik's old town. The rooms have a contemporary, minimalist design, and guests may enjoy panoramic views of the city in the hotel's famous Grillið restaurant.

**For romantic stays:** Within the historic district of Reykjavik, you'll find the lovely residence of the Snowbird, a traditional residence with a variety of one-bedroom apartments perfect for romantic getaways.

**Best for Iceland's second city, Akureyi**

You can get a feel for Icelandic culture in any of the major cities, but Reykjavik is conveniently located near the airport and has an aura of easy coolness about it. Consider the city of Akureyri, which ranks second in population in Iceland despite having a population of fewer than 20,000.

The vibrant city sits at the foot of a fjord in northwest Iceland and is home to world-class skiing as well as a wide variety of eateries and cafés. You can see 30 breathtaking photographs of Iceland, which include the magnificent Akureyrarkirkja cathedral and other breathtaking natural features like Lake Mývatn and Dettifoss.

**Where to stay in Akureyi:**

**For central stays:** To stay in the heart of Akureyrarkirkja, choose Hotel Kea. Guests may enjoy views of Eyjafjördur Fjord from some accommodations, while the hotel's Múlaberg Bistro offers a menu of Icelandic foods with a French twist.

**For cosy stays:** Cozy warmth meets minimalist design at the Icelandair Hotel. With its indoor pool and breathtaking views from most rooms, this hotel is a great choice for ski vacations.

**For budget stays:** Stylish and affordable, the Hafnarstraeti Hostel offers pods for one or two people to sleep in instead of traditional rooms. There is a common kitchen, a store, and barbecue areas in the hostel.

**Best places to stay in Iceland for the northern lights:**

"Up north," you ask? To be honest, there's a solid reason why Iceland is often associated with the northern lights. The much sought-after Aurora Borealis, a colorful, ethereal curtain hanging in the sky, is most likely to be seen between the months of November and March.
You may find hotels all around Iceland that are strategically positioned to see the Northern Lights, provided that you avoid areas with excessive light pollution and are fortunate enough to have clear weather.

**Northern Lights Accommodations:**

**For pampered stays:** Indulge in a luxurious stay at the Hotel Rangá in Hella, where you can make the most of your watching experience with amenities like warm blankets, a balcony that encircles the bar, and wake-up calls at the appropriate times.

**For light-sure stays:** If you are just concerned with seeing the northern lights in Iceland, one of the most reliable options for light-sure accommodations is Hotel Húsafell in Borgarfjordur Valley, which has many displays each week.

**For family stays:** Situated on a horse farm in Iceland, Hótel Lækur in Hella provides a variety of family rooms and a spacious outdoor patio where visitors may see the northern lights during their family vacation.

**Best for dramatic landscapes:**

One of the primaries draws of Iceland is its breathtaking scenery, which includes jagged mountains and gushing waterfalls; hence, it is prudent to remain in close proximity to these natural wonders. Before you leave, make a list of the things you really must see. For ideas, have a look at our guide to the top Iceland attractions.

You can beat the crowds—or at least wait for the tour busses to pull up—by staying near the main attractions. In addition, a few of the nearby hotels are architectural landmarks that merit tourism on their own. See what Copenhagen has to offer in terms of accommodations if that gets you in the mood for Scandi-style.

**Where to stay for dramatic landscapes:**

**For designer stays:** The ION Hotel, located in Thingvellir National Park, is a designer hotel that stands out among the lava fields and rocks. From this location, you may easily access Geysir, Silfra drift, Kerið crater, and the Golden Circle.

**For comfortable stays:** Stylish and cozy, Fosshotel Glacier Lagoon is the perfect place to stay in Vatnajökull National Park, close to the breathtaking Jökulsárlón Glacier Lagoon and Svartifoss Waterfall.

**For unique stays:** For one-of-a-kind lodgings, Iceland offers its own distinctive style: Fjallsarlon Overnight Adventure. It's a collection of yurt-style pods situated on an ice lake close to Selfoss.

**Best for Iceland's geothermal hot springs:**

While they're a welcome relief from the cold in the winter, they're nothing short of opulent in the summer. Regardless of the season, a visit to Iceland's hot springs—fueled by the island's prolific geothermal activity—is a must.

There are many different kinds of springs, from large, well-known ones like the Blue Lagoon to smaller, more secluded pools scattered across rural areas. Check out this list of the best 10 hot springs in Iceland if you're interested in learning more.

**Where to stay for hot springs:**

**For lagoon stays:** Guests of the Blue Lagoon resort may stay in the Silica Hotel. There is a private thermal lagoon just for guests, and the rooms are contemporary and minimalist.

**For romantic stays:** Situated on the coast of the Snaefellsnes peninsula, Hotel Budir is the perfect place for a romantic getaway. Landbrotalaug pool is an intimate hot spring that can accommodate two or three persons, and it serves as an excellent foundation for that.

**For family stays:** The detached Harbour View Cottages are perfect for families; they're located near the Blue Lagoon and include a living room, a terrace with views of the sea, and two bedrooms.

# CHAPTER SIX
## BEST LUXURY HOTELS IN ICELAND

**Hotel Borg:** Looking for a place to stay in the middle of the nation's capital? Consider the Hotel Borg. Hotel Borg, the country's first five-star establishment, has been a top choice for Icelandic travelers for over a century.

The hotel first opened its doors in 1930, catering to the needs of the renowned Icelandic strongman and entertainer Johannes Josefson. Despite many renovations, the building's luxury art-deco interiors and custom-made Cygal furniture are faithful to its heritage.

Situated in one of Reykjavik's most picturesque squares, the hotel is next to both the Icelandic parliament and Domkirkjan, the country's oldest church. A plethora of hip eateries, nightclubs, and boutiques await you the moment you step outdoors.

Choose the Tower Suite when you book your stay at Hotel Borg. A two-story deluxe suite with a separate living area with views of the city below is the biggest accommodation in the hotel.

**Reykjavik Domes:**

A string of unique igloo-shaped lodgings is on display at Reykjavik Domes. These domes may seem like ultra-modern luxury tents from the outside, but this is no average camping vacation. In the domes, you'll find king-size mattresses covered with sheepskin and fully-equipped kitchens, all kept toasty by a crackling fire. Luxurious touches, like as fur throws and private hot tubs, create an atmosphere that is both warm and inviting, and it goes well with the serene environment.

A wide range of activities and personalized trips are also available to visitors at Reykjavik Domes. Prioritizing comfort and elegance, they may set up private transportation to the Golden Circle or further out to the south shore, complete with an English-speaking guide.

**The Retreat at the Blue Lagoon:** One of the most famous landmarks in Iceland is located not far from the city: the Blue Lagoon, a geothermal lagoon of hazy blue encircled by black lava. People travel great distances to see one of Iceland's most photographed locations, the lagoons, with their ethereal, opaque hues and healing, mineral-rich waters.
Its sibling property, The Retreat, began welcoming guests for overnight stays in 2018 at this renowned Icelandic swimming site.

The 62 suites, set on a private inlet next to the world-famous lagoon, provide guests with simple luxury in an attractive style. This health resort radiates seclusion and tranquility with its enormous spa, yoga studio, three eateries, and private entry to the public lagoon.
With its convenient location only twenty minutes from Keflavik Airport, The Retreat may serve as either the beginning or the end of a journey to see the rest of Iceland, or as a home base for seeing the attractions of Reykjavik and the surrounding area.

**Torfhús Retreat:**

The Torfhús Retreat is noted for its skillful combination of genuine Icelandic flair and casual comfort, placing it next on our list of the top hotels in Iceland. Located in the middle of the Golden Circle, this hotel provides amazing views of the Langjokull glacier and snow-capped mountains, as well as convenient access to some of Iceland's most well-known attractions.

Each room at Torfhús and Torfbaer is uniquely designed using local stone and recycled wood, and they all have traditional turf roofs inspired by Icelandic-Viking farms. Accommodations that are evocative of traditional Icelandic accommodations are created by focusing on the country's history and using reused materials. These include items like leathered salmon skins and archive images of historic Torfhúses.

**Hotel Rangá:** We couldn't compile a list of the top Icelandic hotels without including Hotel Rangá. This hotel, which advertises itself as a "northern lights hotel," is situated further south on the island, close enough to black sand beaches and waterfalls to be reached by car.

Thanks to the property's isolation and the consequent lack of light pollution, visitors may marvel at the night sky and witness a plethora of stars, planets, and, on rare occasions, the enchanting northern lights. Guests may take use of the hotel's observatory and powerful telescopes to explore the night sky on guided excursions led by professional astronomers in the area.

The hotel provides an aurora wake-up service so that you won't miss the light display, even if it appears at an ungodly hour, since the presence of the northern lights may be unexpected. You may relax in elegance while watching the aurora borealis in a geothermal hot pool, perhaps with a flute of champagne.

**Deplar Farm, Troll Peninsula:** Guests seeking total solitude will find Deplar Farm to be an ideal home base from which to explore the more distant parts of Iceland. Rather of partaking in the more typical tourist attractions, guests of this 18th-century sheep farm-turned-ultra-luxury hideaway may take advantage of a variety of off-the-beaten-path pursuits, including snow shoeing, heli-skiing, and sea kayaking.

Located on the Troll Peninsula in northern Iceland, this modest retreat offers 13 spacious rooms. In nordic chic rooms decorated with wooden furniture and reindeer-skin rugs, floor-to-ceiling windows embrace the surrounding peaks and vast open sky, casting a warm light throughout.

The outdoors is calling, but many visitors would rather spend their time in the 10,000 square foot spa or relaxing in the luxurious outdoor hot springs. The water of a geothermal pool rises to a swim-up bar situated outside the pool. Before a day of fun-filled activities, guests may try out innovative treatments like isopod flotation tanks to relax in a different way.

**UMI Hotel, Hvolsvollur:** The UMI Hotel is set against the background of one of Iceland's most picturesque mountain ranges. With only 28 beautiful rooms, each with a view of the ocean or mountains, visitors will never feel crowded at this barefoot luxury hotel that has a strong connection to nature in its design, décor, and entire experience. The hotel's first-rate restaurant offers Nordic and Icelandic dishes with a Japanese touch in an inviting setting, while the hotel's lounge and bar are perfect places to take in views of the world-famous subglacial volcano Eyjafjallajökull. The hotel staff can readily organize a variety of exciting activities, such as glacier walks, kayaking, and ice-cave excursions, for visitors who want to experience more than just the breathtaking scenery. This motel is perfect for adventurers and environment lovers!

**Edition Hotel Reykjavik:**

Introducing 5-star luxury to the city, the Reykjavik EDITION is an ideal base for exploring the surrounding area. Just a ten-minute drive will take you to the natural geothermal springs at Sky Lagoon, and the hotel's prime downtown location puts you within walking distance of Laugavegur Street—the city's lively retail district—and the Harpa Concert and Conference Centre. The hotel's contemporary decor is consistent throughout, and guests may choose from a variety of accommodation types, sizes, and views (including those of the harbor and the ocean) to suit their every requirement. From casual snacks to al fresco eating and a more formal dining experience headed by Gunnar Karl Gíslason, the first Michelin-starred chef in Iceland, the hotel offers a range of unique food and drink choices. In addition, there is a fitness center where visitors may get some exercise.  If you're looking for a place to hang out, get some work done, or just have a good time, look no further! The Marriott Collection includes the Edition Hotel Reykjavik.

**Fosshotel Glacier Lagoon:** One stop on every Icelandic road trip should be at Fosshotel Glacier Lagoon, which is situated between Skaftafell and Jökulsárlón Glacier Lagoon. The 125 modern rooms have a serene and uncluttered decor, and their large windows provide breathtaking views of the surrounding nature and Hvannadalshnúkur, the highest mountain in the nation. The hotel's high ceilings contribute to the tranquil atmosphere it offers. With geometric accents and menu items drawn from the hotel's natural setting, the hotel's main restaurant is sure to wow. Of all the great things about this accommodation, the closest one is its location to the Fosshotel Glacier, which offers great trekking just outside your door.

**Hótel Kría:**

In Vik is a good choice for those who are visiting the island's southern region. Located within a five-minute stroll of the area's black sand beaches, this hip newcomer debuted to the public in the summer of 2018. Both the interior and outside of the building showcase contemporary design elements, such as glass, charcoal tones, and light wood paneling. Lamb and fish are the most popular dishes at Drangar Restaurant. At Hótel Kría, you won't want to miss dessert thanks to their innovative pudding menu items including avocado chocolate pudding, skyr and cucumber crystallized white chocolate with dill and merengue.

**Hilton Reykjavik City Centre:**

Staying at the Canopy by Hilton Reykjavik, part of the posh Hilton group, will take care of all your needs throughout your stay in the capital. This unique kind of hospitality is the result of the building's six linked rooms' transformation from a furniture manufacturer and music and arts venue. While staying in one of Canopy's 112 rooms, guests are welcome to examine the vinyl collection and bring their own portable record player (some of which are accessible). Pet-friendly and completely smoke-free, this isn't the spot for smokers, but it's heaven on earth for nonsmokers. There are a number of restaurants there, including the exclusive Geiri Smart, where the menu changes daily to reflect what the area's farmers and fishermen have to offer.

**Alda Hotel:**

Perched on Reykjavik's main retail strip, the Alda Hotel is another popular spot for city breaks. The outdoor hot tub is ideal for relaxing after a day of frenetic touring, and the hotel's focus on serenity and peace creates an oasis-like atmosphere despite its central location. Each of the 88 plush guest rooms has unique decor, including brightly colored walls, original artwork, and designer furniture; each room also comes with a complimentary set of L'Occitane amenities. If you are traveling with children or want a more relaxed style, Alda is the way to go. Brass Kitchen & Bar is a laid-back spot to eat, or you may try some of the many nearby restaurants.

**The Retreat at Blue Lagoon:** Guests at the country's most renowned site may relax in a minimalist room while taking in views of the Blue Lagoon's volcanic wonders at The Retreat at Blue Lagoon. The Retreat Spa is an integral aspect of your stay at The Retreat, and spa vacations are their forte. Lava Cove is an exclusive area inside the main underground spa where the well-to-do may enjoy in-water massages, guided yoga sessions, gourmet meals, and a tranquil atmosphere. Make sure you give the signature ritual a go if you're interested in trying out the seawaters' silica, algae, and mineral content. Another eatery offers a similarly relaxing ambiance. The lagoon, for the traditional Icelandic swim, is also a must-visit.

**ION City Hotel:**

The ION City Hotel is well positioned for nightlife exploration in Reykjavik, with views of the capital's colorful rooftops and the mountains beyond. The rooms at these one of the two ION hotels come with saunas, organic linens, Bang & Olufsen Bluetooth speakers, mid-century furniture, and Scandi style designed by Minarc. At the hotel's restaurant, Sumac, you'll find the cool crowd. Hafsteinn Ólafsson, a renowned chef from Iceland, is in charge of the kitchen, which serves North African cuisine in an atmosphere reminiscent of old Beirut. Unwind with a drink from the bar's interesting selection, which includes Lebanese wine, after your dinner.

**ION Adventure Hotel:** An outstanding example of modernist architecture, the ION Adventure Hotel in Selfoss rests precariously on stilts, creating a striking silhouette against the breathtaking scenery below. This 45-room boutique hotel, which was formerly a haunted inn, offers basic and deluxe rooms with views of the lava fields or the Nesjavellir Geothermal Power Plant. Guests may also enjoy views of Thingvellir National Park. The façade echoes the harsh circumstances of an Icelandic winter, while the inside, like ION's City Hotel, features salvaged materials. The idea and management of the ION brand are by Sigurlaug Sverrisdottir. She used to be flight attendants and now runs a company that plans adventure trips; from this base, you may go on many fantastic adventures. Perched precariously atop Mount Hengill, the Adventure Hotel offers a sustainable haven for those seeking seclusion.

BEST BOUTIQUE HOTELS IN ICELAND

**An Oasis in the Blue Lagoon:**

You may not know this, but there is a stunning boutique hotel in Iceland that looks out over the Blue Lagoon, one of the country's most well-known (and calming!) tourist destinations.

An unforgettable chance to unwind in the lap of luxury in the picturesque setting of Iceland's most exquisite spa is yours at The Retreat at Blue Lagoon. Azure geothermal water encircles the 62 boutique rooms, and the posh Lagoon Suite offers direct access to the water for those fortunate enough to reserve it!

With access to exclusive, exclusive parts of the Retreat Spa that day-trippers aren't allowed to enter, your pinnacle Blue Lagoon experience will be unparalleled regardless of the luxury suite you choose to stay in.

After a day of relaxing in the mineral-rich geothermal waters, treat yourself to a massage, a floating treatment session, or the whole Blue Lagoon Ritual. Or just take in the breathtaking volcanic landscape from the privacy of your suite with floor-to-ceiling windows and a terrace.

The Blue Lagoon has three restaurants where you may savor delicious meals at any time of day. At the Lava Restaurant, a table within an 800-year-old lava cliff offers a view of the Blue Lagoon and a menu of cod, langoustines, and Arctic char.

The Moss Restaurant, which has been recommended by Michelin, is equally atmospheric. Enjoy a tasting meal that rotates with the seasons while gazing out at the moss-covered volcanic landscapes, which are rough and breathtaking.

You can reach The Retreat at Blue Lagoon from both Reykjavik and Keflavik International Airport in a matter of minutes. So, if you're seeking for a handy luxury layover on your trip across the Atlantic, this is one of the finest hotels in Iceland!

**The Borg Hotel:**

Located in the heart of Reykjavik, Hotel Borg is one of the top hotels in Iceland. Guests are sure to be enchanted by the hotel's unique art-deco interior and exterior.

An iconic Icelandic building, Hotel Borg has been welcoming affluent tourists since its grand opening in 1930. If you're looking for a capital city hotel that can lay claim to being Iceland's oldest luxury establishment, go no further than Hotel Borg.

While each of the 99 rooms at Hotel Borg has all the conveniences of a contemporary hotel, they all manage to keep the distinctive art-deco decor that the establishment has been preserving for more than 90 years. The elegant art-deco furniture, the simple hardwood flooring, and the opulent Philippe Starck fixtures will all be to your liking.

In the heart of Reykjavik, on Austurvollur Square, you'll discover the Hotel Borg, which has an unbeatable position and offers stunning views of the cathedral and Icelandic parliament. Your accommodation at the boutique Hotel Borg will provide all the luxury you need after a day of touring in the capital. Another option is to spend the evening indulging in the Borg Spa's saunas, steam rooms, and hot tubs.

**Hotel Tower in Reykjavik:**

Are breathtaking panoramas something you enjoy? Afterwards, your search might end at the charming Tower Suites Reykjavik. With a reservation for a high-end suite in this chic skyscraper, you can be certain that you will be staying in one of the highest buildings in the capital of Iceland, affording you breathtaking views of the harbor and cityscape.

On the twentieth story of this breathtaking skyscraper with a glass exterior are eight luxurious rooms. As soon as you step foot in one of those apartments, you'll be captivated by the room's enormous floor-to-ceiling windows. The in-room telescope allows you to have a better view of the cityscape or the stars.

Tower rooms are very contemporary in feel thanks to their eight individually designed rooms and their smooth wood flooring and open floor plans. Based on their specific placement on the 20th floor, each unit offers a distinct perspective. Views of Mount Keilir and the Snaefellsjokull Volcano may be enjoyed from the Keilir Suite and the Snaefellsjokull Suite, respectively.

**The Geysir Hotel:**

Because of its prime location in the middle of the world-famous Golden Circle, Hotel Geysir is among the most hip hotels in Iceland. The Hotel Geysir's view of the Haukadalur Geothermal region is sure to be a hit with you. The Great Geysir, one of Iceland's most iconic landmarks, is just a few meters away, adding to its allure.

The modern, minimalist architecture of the hotel blends in with the Golden Circle scenery almost imperceptibly. The 77 standard rooms and 6 suites include large windows that look out over the countryside, and the outside is exquisitely elegant. After an exciting day seeing the Golden Circle, unwind in one of the luxurious rooms decorated in soothing earth tones with comfortable furniture.

At the Geysir Restaurant, you can enjoy authentic Icelandic fare like slow-cooked lamb, robust stews, and fresh seafood that changes with the seasons. However, the most amazing thing is the geothermally baked bread. It's really unique and cannot be found anyplace else!

Hotel Geysir is located in the middle of Iceland's rural countryside, but it's just a short drive from Reykjavik. Nearby attractions include Thingvellir National Park, the Gullfoss Waterfall, and a seemingly infinite array of volcanic and glacial landscapes; you're also within walking distance of erupting geysers.

**Budir hotel:**

Hotel Budir is one of our favorite boutique hotels in all of Iceland; it proves that even in the most inaccessible places, Iceland can provide luxurious accommodations. From your comfortable accommodation, you can enjoy breathtaking views of the volcano and the sea, and the hotel is located on the peaceful southern beaches of Snaefellsnes National Park. While the rooms are lovely and have a traditional flair, they lack the modern conveniences you would find at a five-star hotel in Reykjavik. Immerse yourself in nature at Hotel Budir, where you may experience unparalleled serenity and warm hospitality in a secluded corner of the nation.

From your hotel room in the winter, you will definitely be able to see the Northern Lights. Plus, throughout the summer, you may conquer glaciers and go through lava fields to make the most of the long days.

You will be pleasantly delighted to learn that the supper menu at Hotel Budir is surprisingly sophisticated, considering its seclusion. Arctic char, reindeer pate, and other seasonal Icelandic foods are included in the hotel's five-course tasting menu. Enjoy one of Iceland's most comprehensive liquor choices in the hotel bar, and let the in-house sommeliers guide you in the perfect match of wines.

**The Hussafell Hotel:**

Located in the heart of Iceland's Highlands, the secluded boutique hotel Hotel Husafell offers the perfect blend of rustic charm and modern comforts.

At Hotel Husafell, you may choose from 48 boutique rooms. Each room has a minimalist style, natural tones, and artwork by Icelandic artist Páll Guðmundsson. From there, you can enjoy calm views of the countryside.

Unbelievable scenery surrounds Hotel Husafell, and if you visit in the winter, you'll be in the best area to see the Northern Lights dancing across the night sky. The Midnight Sun will captivate you throughout the summer. Glaciers, natural hot springs, and the thundering waterfalls of Iceland are all within easy reach as well!

Even though Hotel Husafell is in a secluded location, it nevertheless has a mini-market where you can buy hiking supplies and a bistro where you can refuel after a day of exploring. Settle down for an elegant evening with a reservation at Husafell Restaurant and savor exquisite Icelandic dishes while taking in breathtaking views of the Highlands.

**Hotel ion adventure:**

Discover boutique luxury in the midst of breathtakingly beautiful scenery at the ION Adventure Hotel, one of the hippest hotels in Iceland.
In the heart of the Golden Circle is the ION Adventure Hotel. From its breathtaking vantage point on Mount Hengill, the hotel offers elegant rooms that look out over Lake Thingvallavatn.

The nearby mountains are covered with snow in the winter, and from the heated outdoor pool, you may stare in wonder at the Northern Lights!

The nearby volcanoes provide the geothermal energy that powers the hotel. Furthermore, the majority of the materials used in the one-of-a-kind design and construction were obtained via sustainable means and recycled. For instance, a lot of the wood is really driftwood, and the hotel's peculiar furnishings even include lava rocks.

All of the hotel rooms have been designed with eco-friendliness in mind as well. Enjoy breathtaking views of the lake, natural herbal toiletries, and minimalist decor.

Fantastic outdoor experiences may be planned by the hotel's personnel, and Thingvellir National Park and the surrounding ice caps and volcanoes are easily accessible. You may unwind in style in the hotel's spa if that is your purpose for being here.

Gourmet dining at the Ion Adventure Hotel is all about "New Nordic Cuisine." Indulge in delicacies like lamb sirloin with rhubarb butter and Arctic char with rye bread and wasabi, which are modern takes on classic Nordic meals.

**Dynheimar Hotel in Akureyri:**

Do you intend to go out into the icy shores of northern Iceland? In such case, the Hotel Akureyri Dynheimar is the place to stay to ensure a cozy (and warm!) vacation. Akureyri is the biggest town in northern Iceland, and this colorful and charming boutique hotel is among the greatest in the area. From here, you can easily reach this faraway region of fire and ice.

Despite its stunning views of the vast fjord that extends northward into the Arctic, the Hotel Akureyri Dynheimar was, shockingly, a movie theater for a long time! The hotel really had one of the first movie theaters in all of Iceland. Movie posters and other memorabilia adorn the walls of this hotel, which pays homage to its rich history and distinctive character.
The Hotel Akureyri Dynheimar is what we call a "cozy," but it's actually a "Microhotel." The Micro Suites are between 11 and 18 square meters in size, but they still have plasma screen TVs, marble bathrooms, luxury beds, and record collections for your listening pleasure.

**Grimsborgir hotel:**

We are the perfect spot for you if you are seeking five-star luxury far from any human settlement. Hotel Grimsborgir is one of the top Icelandic hideaways because each visitor may relax in their own outdoor geothermal hot tub or join a communal one.

All 29 of the hot tubs are in prime locations to relax in mineral-rich water while gazing up at the night sky and the Northern Lights. Since soaking in the hot tub isn't going to cut it, every boutique room, suite, and apartment has its own balcony or terrace as standard.

Because Hotel Grimsborgir is located in the heart of Iceland's Golden Circle, guests can expect to have breathtaking views from their boutique balcony. Great Geysir, Gullfoss, Thingvellir National Park, Kerid Crater, and many more natural wonders are all within easy hiking or driving distance. However, Hotel Grimsborgir remains distant, lonely, and cut off from the outside world, even though it is located near some of Iceland's most famous outdoor tourist sites.

The Nordic country of Iceland is known for its protein-rich yogurt, skyr, and for its daily buffet breakfasts that include cured meats, cheeses, and the local delicacy.

The hotel restaurant has a rotating lunch and supper menu that changes with the seasons and uses products that are acquired locally. They can even make you a packed lunch to take with you on your holiday. The vegan Wellington, the fully piled "Grimsburger," and the Icelandic meat soup are some of the menu's highlights.

**Magma hotel!**

From its secluded location off the Ring Road in southeast Iceland, Hotel Magma commands breathtaking views of black sand beaches, lava fields, and volcanic peaks—a name befitting this one-of-a-kind boutique hotel.

For these and many more reasons, the Magma Hotel is among the most hip hotels in Iceland. The eco-friendly cabins at the hotel feature moss-covered roofs and are furnished with elegant Nordic elegance that combines plenty of practicality with maximum warmth.

A straight line from the finest cottages' outside terraces to the lake below is a given. In addition, from any point on the Magma Hotel grounds, you can see the distant peak of Vatnajokull, the biggest ice cap in Iceland.

Bistro 1783 serves home-cooked meals with breathtaking views of Vatnajokull. The magma hotel sits on the enormous lava field formed by the eruption of the Lakagigar Volcano in the year that the restaurant was named after that event. For morning, you may have eggs, bacon, and fresh fruit with some Icelandic skyr. As for supper, the menu changes with the seasons and what's in season.

**Umi hotel area:**

Book a boutique break at UMI Hotel and stay in the shadow of one of the most infamous volcanoes in the world. One of the nicest hotels in Iceland, and not only because the hotel bar is rich and well-stocked and offers a breathtaking view of the incomprehensible Eyjafjallajokull volcano.

Remember Eyjafjallajokull? It was the volcano that erupted in 2010 and blocked most European aviation travel for weeks due to the massive ash clouds that engulfed the sky. Conveniently situated on the south coast of Iceland, UMI Hotel is only a mile off the famed Route 1 highway and is in the shadow of Eyjafjallajokull.

Guests are sure to be as impressed by the sleek hotel's dark, brooding, and beautifully modern appearance as they are by the stunning nearby countryside. The UMI Hotel is owned by a family, and if you're fortunate, you could meet Breki, the hotel dog, who likes to meet visitors when they arrive!

The UMI Hotel is a small boutique with only 28 rooms, and each one is decorated in a dark and gloomy style to reflect the volcanic landscapes of Iceland. In addition, every one of them has a breathtaking view of the sea or the mountains. Guests can always count on the hotel's top-notch restaurant to wow with its ever-changing menu that features a delightful fusion of Nordic, Icelandic, and Japanese flavors.

**Rancho Santa Fe:**

Hotel Ranga is the spot to go if you're a fan of the rustic Icelandic log cabin style but yet want an opulent vacation. The outside is rustic logs and the inside is smooth timbers, giving this four-star luxury getaway the look of a Nordic winter hut.

We guarantee that you will love the one-of-a-kind boutique rooms decorated with vibrant murals and individually selected furniture. Beautiful views of the Icelandic landscape, including Mount Hekla and the Ranga River, are yours to enjoy from the comfort of your hotel accommodation.

Relax in the outdoor hot tubs' geothermally heated water while taking in the breathtaking views of the Northern Lights.

## BEST CHEAP & MID-RANGE HOTELS IN ICELAND

One of the best places on Earth to visit is, of course, Iceland. The ring road is a sight to see for first-time visitors, who gaze in awe at the primordial landscapes that are being shaped right before their eyes. These landscapes may seem ancient to us, but they are really quite new compared to other nations on Earth. People who go to this nation again and again explore its lesser-known regions, living in the little communities that cling to the cliffs, going on long hikes, and finding that every valley, fjord, and mountain heath has its own unique beauty.

An overwhelming sense of wonder is what all visitors to this remote North Atlantic Island share from their travels across the nation. In contrast to the exciting sights and sounds outside, the hotels dotting the nation provide tranquil havens where guests may unwind in style. These are the top hotels in Iceland, ranging from cozy rural cabins to chic Scandinavian retreats.

**The process we use to choose the finest Icelandic hotels**
The editors of Condé Nast Traveler have personally stayed at each hotel on this list, and each review is written by a writer with first-hand knowledge of the area. Luxury establishments, boutique hotels, and hidden gems that provide an insider's look at a place are all considered by our editors when making hotel recommendations. In addition to strong sustainable credentials, we are always on the hunt for stunning design, an ideal location, and friendly service. We make sure to keep this list up-to-date when new hotels are added and old ones change.

**Reykjavik Edition:**

Located in the heart of Reykjavik, the newest hotel on the block, the Reykjavik Edition, is a welcome change of pace in this artistic and fashion-forward metropolis. This hotel, which is part of Marriott's highly sought-after Edition brand and was designed by Ian Schrager, elevates Reykjavik to the same level as other prestigious locations such as Shanghai, Manhattan, Barcelona, and Tokyo.

The Reykjavik Edition is typical of the group's hotels in that it reflects the local culture. Materials such as basalt, lava, warm wood, and concrete wonderfully capture the young and dynamic vibe of Reykjavik, while the décor has bursts of Nordic ingenuity balanced by a clean and uncomplicated style. The rooms are then filled with Italian ash wood furniture and have floor-to-ceiling windows that look out over the fjord, Mt. Esja, or Reykjavik's city. The setting is picture perfect, nestled between Reykjavik's Old Harbour and the majestic Harpa Concert Hall. This is the best hotel in Iceland when you include a rooftop terrace where you can see the northern lights, a restaurant managed by the country's first Michelin-starred chef, Gunnar Karl Gíslason, and a cozy bar in the manner of a speakeasy.

**Hotel Rangá:**

Guests are welcomed by Hrammur the polar bear, a 10-foot-tall taxidermy that met an untimely end on Iceland's beaches after drifting across from Greenland. The hotel is located in the south of Iceland. This south coast hotel, which is equal parts opulent hunting lodge and exciting rural house, uses it as its welcome statement. If you're looking for a peaceful retreat in the heart of southern Iceland, this log cabin is the perfect choice. Just look inland at the twin glaciers Eyjafjallajökull and Mýrdalsjökull, and you'll feel the adventure calling you as you step out the front door.

Warm, welcoming, and sociable, Hotel Ranga is the perfect place to unwind after a day of exploring—maybe on the glacier in a snowmobile or on a private super jeep tour of the mysterious Thórsmörk Nature Reserve. The apartments have a warm, welcoming vibe reminiscent of an Icelandic summer cottage, and the common areas are decorated with artwork and blankets made in the area. The seven luxurious suites are a standout feature; they are themed after the seven continents that stretch from Antarctica to the Americas. In addition to the obligatory hot tub for an evening dip, there is a world-class observatory where you can meet a local astronomer who can also take pictures of the northern lights and show you how to get the perfect shot of the aurora borealis in all its dazzling glory.

**The Retreat at Blue Lagoon**

On the Reykjanes Peninsula, in the hot blue water surrounded by black lava, is the Blue Lagoon, one of the most famous tourist spots in Iceland. Every day, a steady flow of tourists comes to swim in the lagoon. Because of its popularity, Icelandic tourists are sharply divided into two groups: those who wish to avoid the typical tourist traps and those who go all out. Would you recommend going to the Blue Lagoon or would you rather not? Well, that's the rub.

Staying at the posh new hotel connected to Iceland's famous hot spring would be an easy question to answer. With its cryptic moniker, "The Retreat," this hotel transforms the Blue Lagoon's geothermal beauty into an ultra-luxurious spa. With floor-to-ceiling windows that let in the ethereal light of the Reykjanes Peninsula, the harsh grey and muted black interiors are induced into a heady and mystical Icelandic spectrum, while the sleek and minimalist rooms reflect the mossy-covered lava fields outside. The subterranean spa is accessible via any of the interior corridors; it is a vast room that provides the unique Blue Lagoon Ritual, a health cleansing that makes use of the silica, algae, and variety of minerals contained in the geothermal waters. Not only that, but there's a world-class restaurant and access to a private portion of the Blue Lagoon.

**ION Adventure Hotel:**

The ION Adventure Hotel has a location that rivals any in the Northern Hemisphere in terms of beauty and otherworldliness. Within the UNESCO-recognized Thingvellir National Park, this hotel is perched among whirling sulfurous steam, protruding from a series of craggy cliffs that overlook a field of jet-black lava. The interiors are a haven of comfort and peace, in stark contrast to the rather striking exterior. Incorporating driftwood and other natural elements from the surrounding landscapes, the sleek design creates a fusion of high-end luxury with understated Icelandic sensibility, paying tribute to the breathtaking surroundings outside.

The Northern Lights Bar stands out; it overlooks the lava field and has enormous windows where you can see the aurora borealis dancing across the sky. Indulge in delectable delicacies like glazed lamb shank and fresh Arctic char at the onsite Silfra Restaurant, and take in the breathtaking weather of Iceland from the comfort of a heated plunge pool that is elegantly exposed to the elements. Additionally, the hotel is an excellent jumping off point for more in-depth tours of the Golden Circle. Guests may arrange a wide variety of activities via reception, including super-jeep excursions of the glaciers, snorkeling between the Silfra rift, and explorations into adjacent lava caves.

**Deplar Farm:**

The Tröllaskagi Peninsula is an excellent option for tourists who want to go away from the ring road and see the rural areas of Iceland. A solitary route winds down the rocky shoreline of one of the country's most hilly regions, linking several fishing villages that are dwarfed by the enormous landscape and offering glimpses of the breathtaking Northern Atlantic Ocean. Deplar Farm is located in one of the valleys that cut through the fog-kissed mountains in the interior. One of the most secluded and exquisite mountain hotels in Europe is in a grassy meadow surrounded by majestic peaks. The turf-covered farmhouse is so modest and peaceful that the occasional traveler who does happen to pass by would never guess.

Deplar Farm provides daring tourists with the whole experience, and it's run by the exclusive and high-end Eleven Experience. In the winter, guests may enjoy heli-skiing, while in the summer, they can go mountain biking or salmon fishing with the help of the hotel's professional guides. Upon your return, you will find a heated pool with a swim-up bar, cozy, stylish accommodations that overlook the tranquil meadow, and world-class cuisine produced by a team of great Icelandic chefs.

**Hotel Egilsen:**

With its glistening harbor, rugged cliffs, prim old buildings painted a different color, and snow-dusted mountains towering in the distance, the village of Stykkishólmur on the Snaefellsnes Peninsula is one of the most gorgeous in all of Iceland, according to Hotel Egilsen. As you meander around the town, it's not hard to picture the trading ships from Norway, Sweden, and Denmark docking at the harbor. This town was really a major port during the most prosperous period of commerce in Scandinavia, which lasted from the 17th to the 19th century.

Constructed by a prosperous Icelandic trader and businessman in 1867, the historic mansion where the Hotel Egilsen now stands is a remnant of that era. The bright red facades are sure to catch your eye, concealing a charming boutique hotel that exudes nostalgia and offers a cozy Nordic experience. During your visit, you can anticipate rooms decorated with sea and fishing-themed decor, a mix of antique and modern pieces, and a comforting sense of belonging. Additionally, the hotel has an enticing library filled with ancient Nordic folk stories and poems from Iceland. Guests are invited to record their own stories while they are here, with the majority of them being influenced by the breathtakingly gorgeous Snæfellsnes Peninsula, and they will then be shared on the hotel's website.

**101 Hotel:**

We strongly suggest the 101 Hotel in Reykjavik to creative travelers who want to see the country's design sector at its peak. Reykjavik is a city that runs on creativity. One of the most esteemed properties in the Design Hotels collection, 101 Hotel has ostentatiously chic and confidently modern decor. A collection of modern Icelandic artworks graces the stark black and white rooms, which are furnished with exquisite pieces that exude an air of easy designer elegance.

Inviting and homey, the rooms have plush mattresses, carpets scattered over hardwood flooring, and a view of Mt. Esja from the ocean. Indulge in a meal at the on-site restaurant, which has a loyal following among locals. After a day of seeing Reykjavik, unwind with a glass at the elegant bar, where seats are arranged around tree-trunk tables and a warm fireplace. All of this is conveniently located just off Laugavegur, the main drag of the city.

**Hotel Flatey:**

From Stykkishólmur, tourists have the option to board the Westfjords ferry, which takes its time navigating the Breiðafjörður fjord and stops at a port on the southern coast of Iceland's least-visited area, past many boulders, skerries, and islands. On the other side, the boat mysteriously docks at Flatey, the only inhabited island in the fjord—a nostalgic spot with a few brightly painted cottages scattered about. Even if you just spend one night at the island hotel, you will feel as if you have slipped into the discordant cadence of an Icelandic summer. As you wander aimlessly, as many tourists do in Iceland, you'll see birdsong, shimmering grass, and a warm, golden light casting a warm glow over the rocky coasts and neighboring seascapes.

There are only around five people living on the island during the winter, therefore the modest Hotel Flatey is only open during the summer. Guests may enjoy nice accommodations spread out among many residences from the 19th century. With a minimalist style right out of a design magazine, the interiors are romantically Scandinavian. The hotel restaurant doubles as the island's bar and lounge, where summer visitors and residents alike congregate for a hearty dinner and lively conversation. Everything about it is as hospitable as visiting a long-lost Icelandic relative's house.

**The Balúðir Hotel:**

One of the most appealing aspects of Iceland is the opportunity to experience complete solitude among breathtaking natural scenery, which may make one feel small and threatened. As a result of the breathtaking grandeur of nature, we often find ourselves trembling in our hiking boots. Because it evokes emotions we don't often get the chance to experience, Iceland has quickly become one of the world's most visited countries.

That characteristic is fully embraced by the top hotels in Iceland, which provide sophisticated settings that allow the scenery to speak for itself. Nestled on a secluded beach on the southern coast of the Snæfellsnes Peninsula, Hotel Búðir is one such establishment. The captivating Icelandic landscapes around this former Danish trade station, drawing your attention from the views over the harbor to the gloomy glacier in the heart of Snæfellsnes National Park. A fantastical setting with tasteful, understated furnishings that echo the ethereal atmosphere outdoors. In addition to the restaurant's fame among Icelanders, the property's vintage-style furnishings give it an air of timeless beauty.

**Kvosin Downtown Hotel:**

In the heart of downtown Reykjavik, in a charming boutique property with great apartment suites, you'll find the Kvosin Hotel. This hotel is perfect for a long stay in Reykjavik since it combines urban and Nordic flair, has friendly personnel, and is located in the heart of the city. Buildings in Iceland tend to be older than a century, which is fitting given the abundance of historic landmarks in the area, including the cathedral, the Icelandic parliament, and the City Hall.

Using a more contemporary version of Reykjavik as its inspiration, Kvosin tells a whole other tale on the inside. The newly refurbished furnishings are contemporary and stylish, making them an ideal home base for exploring the nation's capital. Just a short distance from the hotel, you'll find a variety of entertainment options, including live music, craft beer, and the city's center pond, Tjörnin, where you can relax and take a walk. Stylish leather seats, modern kitchenettes, and attractive tables for journaling await you as you stumble home from Reykjavik's vibrant nightlife.

## BEST HOSTELS IN ICELAND

Among the world's nations, Iceland ranks high for its breathtaking beauty and majesty. It is not surprising that this island is adored by those who come, given its mesmerizing waterfalls, bizarre lava fields, beaches with black sand, and majestic volcanic peaks. Nobody I've ever met didn't have affection for their country.
Choosing a hostel is no easy feat, so let's take our time and think about all the factors. What makes a decent hostel outstanding is something I've learnt after more than ten years of globetrotting. According to the research,

**The four most important aspects are:**

**Location:** The geographical dispersion of Iceland makes getting around a bit of a chore. Find a spot that's close to all the tourist attractions and exciting nightlife areas you wish to visit. You won't find any of these hostels in any less central locations.

**Budget:** In Iceland, quality is more important than price, so be prepared to get a crowded, poorly serviced hostel if you go for a less expensive option.

**Facilities:** Free Wi-Fi and breakfast are standard at most hostels, but if you're looking for more, you'll have to do some digging to find the perfect place!

**Staff:** The hostels that are featured here all have fantastic staff members! Their expertise and friendliness are second to none. Look up reviews to make sure you wind up someplace with helpful and pleasant personnel, even if you don't stay at one of the locations mentioned here! an whole hostel could depend on them!

My top picks for Icelandic hostels are below for your perusal as you plan out your vacation. Without breaking the bank, you may find a warm and welcoming spot to rest your head, meet other travelers, and recharge your batteries at any of these options.

**KEX Hostel (Reykjavik):**

"Kex" means "biscuit" or "cookie" in Icelandic, and this 200-person hostel is located in what was formerly a biscuit factory. Various accommodation options are available in the massive Scandi-industrial-chic environment, including private double rooms, rooms that may accommodate families, dormitories that are exclusively for females, and mixed-gender dorms. You are need to provide your own lock for the dormitories' lockers.

You'll meet many of interesting individuals at this hostel, especially in the bar area. Artists and designers also make the complex their permanent home, which gives it a cool, artistic vibe. A kitchen and a heated outdoor patio are available. Also, getting about the city is a breeze because to its convenient location.

**KEX in a nutshell**

Hip-hop interior design and style

Feels like home away from home in an unusually pleasant manner

Insider tips from Reykjavik's tour gurus

Private rooms start at 16,000 ISK and beds cost 4,140 ISK.

**The Freezer (Snaefellsbær):** The Freezer, located in Snaefellsbær, is a hostel common area furnished with sofas.

With just four rooms and the capacity to host twenty-two guests, The Freezer in Snæfellsbær, west Iceland, isn't exactly a sprawling establishment. While it may be little, the amount of enjoyment it offers more than compensates. Anyone may meet interesting people and have a good time at our artistic, relaxed hostel. During happy hour (6–8 pm), the in-house tiki bar becomes even livelier. The common spaces are well-stocked with board games, and you can find film screenings, pub quizzes, and live music on a regular basis on the program.

Not much to rave about in terms of the mattresses, but the rooms are bright and there's a kitchen for those who want to whip up some meals. The price also covers the linen.

**A quick look in the freezer:**

Fantastic on-site tiki bar that hosts fantastic happy hour

Pleasant atmosphere

Happenings every night

Starting from 3,850 ISK for beds and 22,000 ISK for private rooms.

**Akureyri Backpackers (Akureyri):**

You are now viewing the Akureyri Backpackers website. Gathering place for visitors and backpackers, with sofas for relaxation

This hostel is as vibrant as it gets in the northern town of Akureyri, situated in the heart of town close to restaurants, cafes, and pubs. Burgers, nachos, and other non-Icelandic comfort foods are available in the in-house bar, where you can also find a selection of local beers on tap. The three-story facility has 103 beds spread over private rooms, mixed-gender dormitories, and single-gender dorms. There are lockers and quite large rooms, however the mattresses are simple and not very comfortable. There is a sauna in addition to the fully-equipped kitchen!

**Arrival in Akureyri Quick facts for hikers: sauna**

Vibrant on-site pub

Optimistic mood

Prices start at 6,400 ISK for a bed and go up to 4,600 ISK for a private room.

**Bus Hostel (Reykjavik):**

This contemporary hostel is located in a residential area, not on an old bus, and has no connection to buses whatsoever, despite the name. It is around a fifteen-minute walk from the

heart of Reykjavik. However, its proximity to the major bus terminal makes it an ideal stop for travelers heading to and from the airport.

There are individual rooms, female-only dormitories, and mixed dorms. One unusual feature of Icelandic hostels is that they provide linens as well. Buzz, the on-site bar, serves you a variety of four different beers, so you may choose and choose which ones to try. Clean, contemporary, and with great water pressure in the showers, the restrooms are a real treat. Even if it gets crowded, the kitchen is good; hence, if you want to cook, you need get there early.

**An overview of the Bus Hostel:**

Proximity to the major bus terminal makes airport transportation a breeze.

relaxed attitude

Excellent on-site bar

Private rooms start at 18,000 ISK, while beds start at 6,800 ISK.

**Hafnarstræti Hostel (Akureyri):**

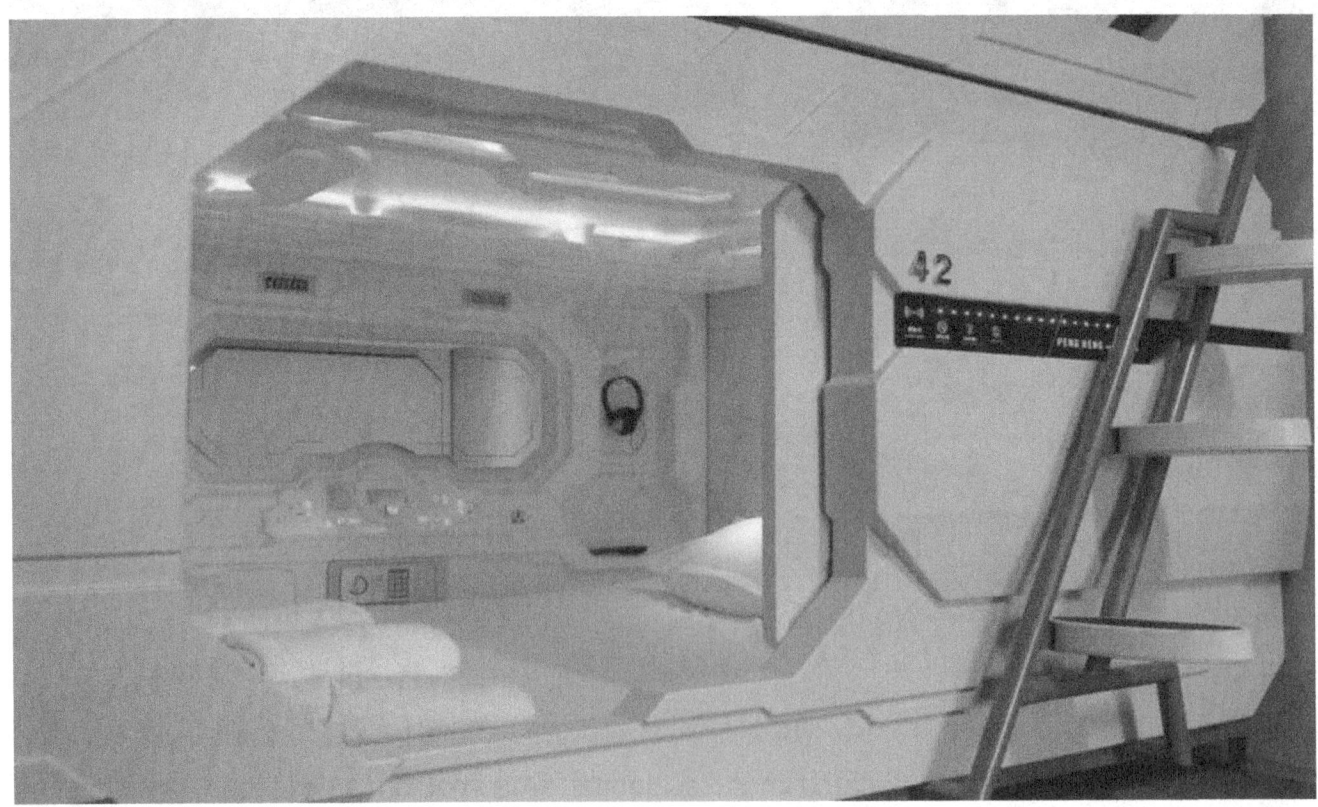

For those seeking a more science-fictional experience during their stay in Iceland, this contemporary hostel offers capsule rooms. You will not share a bed with anybody else in the dorm, but rather have your very own self-contained pod that can be sealed shut so you can sleep soundly. Plugs, storage, and a TV screen are all amenities included in the quite roomy pods. Not only are the bathrooms spotless, but the mattresses are also quite cozy.

Spend your free time playing billiards and board games with other guests in the large common area while you're not in your pod.

**A quick look at Hafnarstræti Hostel:**

Pleasant common area Silent ambiance

Cozy and pleasant pod rooms

Starting at 7,500 ISK for beds and 13,000 ISK for capsule beds.

**Loft HI Hostel (Reykjavik):**

This Reykjavik establishment has high expectations after being named the world's greatest hostel. Plus, it lives up to expectations. You will like lounging about in the room for a while since the dorms and private rooms are comfortable enough. Though simple, the dorm bunks are rather comfortable, with substantial mattresses.

In some rooms, you may enjoy breathtaking views of the city. The rooftop terrace is a great spot to meet other tourists if that doesn't work for you. Evening activities like live music and stand-up comedy are often hosted by the hostel, and the staff is always willing to assist with any inquiries or trip planning you may have.

**An overview of the Loft HI Hostel:**

The Loft HI Hostel is known for its rooftop terrace and breathtaking views.

Concerts, stand-up comedy, and other regular nighttime activities

Pleasant accommodations

Starting at 7,500 ISK for a bed and 32,500 ISK for a private room.

**Lækur Hostel (Reykjavik):**

The warm springs that flow near Lækur, which is a hostel in Reykjavik, are the reason for its name. Numerous rooms are available, including private ones with one, two, or three beds, as well as eight-bed dormitories. The mattresses are cozy, but there are no curtains on the bunks. However, each bunk has its own power outlet and lighting. You may want to make your own dinner every night in the spacious and well-appointed communal kitchen, thanks to the stylish and immaculate bathrooms; but, the Nordic-themed café does provide some delicious options as well.

**Quick overview of Lækur Hostel:**

Chic café with a Nordic motif

Delicious morning meal Stylish and modern decor

Prices for beds start at 8,600 ISK.

**Grundarfjördur Hostel (Grundarfjördur):**

Snæfellsnes Glacier National Park is said to have mystical characteristics, and Grundarfjördur Hostel is a good starting point for visiting this park. Although the dormitories are located all throughout the little town, the hostel's two-story crimson structure serves as the lobby and reception.

Clean, roomy rooms with simple but comfortable bunk beds are available, as is a kitchenette for those who want to prepare their own meals. Although the decor and artwork are a little old, the hostel is still really pleasant and well located. In addition to the great views, several of the accommodations provide views of the world-famous Kirkjufell, also known as Church Mountain.

**Description of Grundarfjördur Hostel:**

Fun for the whole family

Gorgeous setting

Charming living area

Prices start at 14,300 ISK for a twin room and go up to 20,000 ISK for a quad room. Please be informed that at this time, private rooms cannot be reserved for use in dormitories.

**Hafaldan HI Hostel – Old Hospital (Hafaldan):**

This inviting hostel is located in what was formerly a hospital, as the name indicates. Extra-comfortable accommodations and a spa (complete with a sauna!) are available.

Their lodging options range from dormitories to private apartments, two-person rooms, and four-bed private rooms, with or without common bathrooms. There is a noticeable difference between the private room beds and the dorm ones. Anyway, the rooms are tidy, the bathrooms are pristine, and the showers are powerful.

**Just a quick rundown of Hafaldan HI Hostel in the Old Hospital:**

Relax in the on-site sauna

Excellent site

Bedding starts at 5,400 ISK and private rooms are 10,500 ISK. The staff is friendly.

# CHAPTER SEVEN
## 11 MUST EAT PLACES IN ICELAND: WHERE TO EAT IN 2024

In Iceland, you may discover a wide variety of mouth-watering foods. The restaurants in Iceland provide only the finest cuisine, whether it's traditional fare or more modern bistro fare.

**Strikid:**

Bokullupizza, a white pizza topped with beef, bernaise sauce, cheese, and french fries, is served on a white dish at Strikid (Strikið), widely regarded as one of Iceland's greatest restaurants.

Page number fourteen, Akureyri 600, Iceland

Link: Strikid

Located smack dab in the center of Akureyri, Iceland is Strikid. For hikers who would rather not base themselves in the nation's capital, this is a popular location. It's a popular spot that's easy to get to, and it offers great food and beautiful views.

For a really enchanted dining experience, try eating outside in the summer while gazing out at the fjord. A wide selection of grilled and sushi-style fish is available. Beef, chicken, and vegetarian alternatives are also available. In addition to a great atmosphere, they provide a decent drink selection. If you find yourself in Iceland again, you may want to give Strikid a try.

**Kef Restaurant:**

The Kef Restaurant in the Hotel Keflavik is among the greatest restaurants in Iceland, and it serves three tacos on top of a black pate with lime.

The address is Hotel Iceland, Vatnsnesvegi 12, Keflavik, Reykjanesbaer 230, Iceland.

Web Address: Kef Dining Room

Kef Restaurant serves absolutely mouth-watering cuisine. making traditional, beloved foods utilizing items from the area, such as tacos and salads. If you're in the mood for something heartier, such beef tenderloin, there are bigger dinners available.

The servings are really substantial, however. The Kef Restaurant is said to be very popular. You should definitely book ahead of time if you plan on visiting during their busiest dinner times or on weekends. Once you have a seat, the service will be second to none. In most cases, your food will be ready in no time at all.

**Rain:**

Address: Hafnargata 19, Keflavik, Reykjanesbaer 230, Iceland Canary Islands

Website: Rain

The beautiful Icelandic shore is seen from Rain's large, breathtaking windows. After a hard day, it's the perfect spot to relax. You can still have a few of cocktails while gazing out at the bay, even if you're not really hungry.

The bay is just lovely. You are fortunate if hunger strikes you. Rain is a seafood expert. At all times, the fish is succulent and tasteful. Plus, it has great sides, like potato mash, on the side. Lobster soup or a shared serving of fish and chips are two great appetizer choices. One great thing about Rain is that you are free to spend as much time as you like without being asked to cease it. It's the perfect place to unwind.

**Salatsjoppan:**

This is Salatsjoppan, one of the top restaurants in Iceland, serving a black platter of fresh mixed vegetables.

This is the address: Tryggvabraut 22, Akureyri 600; Iceland

Digital address: Salatsjoppan

If you're in need of a charming setting to have your midday snack, Salatsjoppan is the one for you. Everything about this restaurant is its atmosphere. It exudes an air of refined coziness. On top of that, the service is impeccable, and the employees are well-versed in all of the dishes.

It would take a lot of willpower to ruin the fun. Not only are the costs low, but the ambiance and cuisine are second to none. The restaurant's prime location in the middle of Akureyri is an added bonus.

**Bautinn:**

This burger and fries combo from one of Iceland's top eateries, Bautinn, comes on a plate with gray spots.

The exact address is 92 Hafnarstraeti, Akureyri 600, Iceland.

Go to: Bautinn

Bautinn is another hidden treasure in Akureyri that offers delicious comfort cuisine. Along with enormous burritos, salads, and chimichangas. In the aftermath of a day of walking across Iceland, Bautinn is a great alternative if you're looking for a fast meal.

This restaurant does seem to become rather crowded. Therefore, you may want to think about reserving a table. Particularly if you plan to travel during a more popular period.

Everyone from carnivores to vegetarians may find something to their liking. If you're not very hungry, you can always have an appetizer to split. Both the focaccia and the potato wedges are delicious.

**Ilmur Kaffi:**

Address: 107 B Hafnarstraeti, Akureyri 600, Iceland

Link: Kaffi Ilmur

You may get great coffee and delicious food at this establishment. You won't find a more picturesque place in Iceland to have a delicious lunch. The star of the show is the freshly prepared and steaming coffee.

A few of cups will set you up for a delicious walk or adventure. If you're in the mood for some delicious food and have some time to spare, Kaffi Ilmur has an impressive selection.

Fresh sandwiches and creative lamb soup are just a few of the tasty options. When you're very starving, try some of the smoked lamb or roast beef. Try the veggie quiche if you're on a diet and save space for dessert.

**Greifinn:**

One of the greatest restaurants in Iceland, Greifinn, serves you delicious Pizza Nautabanans with coffee.

Glerargata 20, Akureyri 600, Iceland

Location: Greifinn

People love to eat at this eatery. Thus, plan ahead and book your appointments as soon as possible. People from all around, including visitors, like this reasonably priced gem.

Not to mention that there are often intriguing new meals added to the menu. Greifinn has the most amazing fish. Additionally, the pizzas are excellent if you are seeking something lighter or to split with a friend.

Traditional American fare like burgers, large salads, and great beverages are also available. You may receive delicious, reasonably priced cuisine at this reputable restaurant.

**Retturinn:**

The address is 51 Hafnargotu, Keflavik, Reykjanesbaer, Iceland.

Location: Retturinn

If you are in search of delicious and genuine Icelandic food, Retturinn in Keflavik is a great place to go. Soup, parsley potatoes, traditional pork, and meatballs are just a few of the many classic dishes available.

Be ready to wait if you go since it's a tiny establishment and it's only open for a few restricted hours. There's no regret. The portions are large enough to split, and the prices are reasonable. At certain periods of the year, you may also purchase combination dinners. Also, it's not uncommon for them to run one or two promotions simultaneously. When you notice that the locals are heading there, you'll know it's amazing.

**Apotek Restaurant:**
Address: 1600 Austurstraeti, Reykjavik, 101 Iceland
Website: The Apotek Restaurant
You won't regret visiting Apotek Restaurant in Iceland's capital city. There is an extensive menu at this upscale eatery.
Meaning you may try some typical Icelandic dishes or branch out and try some new ones. You get to decide. Remember to order many plates and be ready to share the delicious meal when you arrive. Foie gras, french fries, preserved meats, salmon, and massive ribeye steaks are among their most popular meals.
You must try their drinks. However, if you'd rather not indulge, they also have excellent cappuccinos. Apotek Restaurant is known for its fantastic crowds and sometimes live music.

**Old Iceland Restaurant:**

At Old Iceland Restaurant, widely regarded as one of Iceland's finest dining establishments, a skilled chef delicately slices a salted steak on a rustic wooden chopping board.

Site address: 72 Laugavegur, Reykjavik 101, Iceland

This is the Old Iceland Restaurant WEBSITE.

Tourists and locals alike flock to this highly acclaimed eatery in Reykjavik. Make your reservation before 6 o'clock in the afternoon, but if you show there later, you may have to wait.

When the meal finally arrives, however, the majority of customers agree that it was well worth the wait. Delicious alternatives including fish, lamb, salmon, and sweets created just that way are available on the set menu.

It doesn't seem overly crowded, despite the restaurant's little size. Rather, you will get the impression that you are having dinner with friends. Old Iceland Restaurant also welcomes customers who are gluten intolerant or have food allergies.

**Fiskfélagid – Fish Company:**

A meal at Fish Company (Fiskfélagid), one of Iceland's top restaurants, is presented with utensils on a napkin.

Site: 2a Vesturgata Grófartorg, Reykjavik 101, Iceland

The Fiskfelagid Fish Company website

The name gives it away: the seafood at this eatery is second to none. Because of this, you will probably find what you're searching for, whether it's more traditional food or something completely new and exciting.

You may also order from the chef's menu or come up with your own creative surf and turf. When it comes to plating and presentation, this restaurant is unparalleled. The moment you take a seat, you will realize you have entered a unique place.

Looking over the menu, it's hard to imagine picking a terrible meal. Nevertheless, the fresh fish of the day, tuna tartare, scallop and lobster soup, and other dishes stand out. In order to make the most of your experience, it is recommended to order many meals to share.

**Reykjavík Kitchen:**

A wooden table at Reykjavík Kitchen, renowned as one of the top restaurants in Iceland, displays a bowl of classic Kjotsupa Icelandic Lamb Soup, accompanied with a spoon and other dishes in the background.

Raudararstig 8, Reykjavik 105, Iceland

Reykjavik Kitchen's website

Reykjavik Kitchen is conveniently located in the heart of Reykjavik. Almost all of the main hotels and landmarks are in close proximity. Therefore, you are welcome to drop by after your day of touring or trekking is over.

Everyone working there is kind and very knowledgeable about the menu. If you have any dietary constraints, they may also provide ideas. Nothing beats freshly baked bread. Plus, you need to give it a go with the classic accompaniments: whipped butter and unusual salt. The cured meats and seafood are the best part of the meal. Grilled fish and lamb are examples of heartier dishes.

**Matarkjallarinn – Foodcellar:**

One of the top restaurants in Iceland, Matarkjallarinn, serves glazed lamb fillet on a white platter with potatoes and a port sauce.
The address is Adalstraeti 2, Reykjavik 101, Iceland.
Matarkjallarinn-Foodcellar is the website.

The Matarkjallarinn Foodcellar is located in the middle of the city in a historic structure. As an added bonus, eating there is an unforgettable and unforgettable experience. Expertly matched, they employ a wide variety of regional ingredients.

They pair them with drinks that are both traditional and quirky. It's the kind of elegant but welcoming eatery that will deepen your love for Iceland. Duck and lamb, among other meats, are excellent here.

Vegetarian options and delicious sweets are also available. On occasion, a pianist will serenade you while you dine. For the timetable, see their website. Get ready to be astounded.

**The Coocoo's Nest:**

One of the top restaurants in Iceland, The Coocoo's Nest, serves whole zucchini sourdough pizza.

Address: 23 Grandagardur Street, Reykjavik, 101 Iceland

Address: The Coocoo's NestWebsite

One of your favorite restaurants in Reykjavik is sure to be this laid-back spot with a cool vibe. Tacos and pizza, for example, are tasty and unpretentious options. However, each dish is prepared to a flawless finish.

There is an excellent assortment of creative drinks made using regional ingredients at the Coocoo's Nest. Indulge in breathtaking views of the waterfront while you dine here.

The service is prompt, kind, and expert. Simply inquire with the staff if you have any issues or queries about the menu. Additionally, you have the option to make changes as needed, and sometimes, they do have sales.

**Restaurant Aura:**

One of the top restaurants in Iceland, Restaurant Aura, serves beef bourguignon on a white dish.

Building 2 at Reykjanesbaer 235 in Iceland (Blikavollur 2)

Online: Aura Restaurant

If you're in the mood for some delicious seafood, go no further than Restaurant Aura. Their creative and delicious preparations give the impression that the ingredients are plucked straight from the sea.

If you ask one of their waiters, they can recommend the perfect wine or drink to go with your meal. As a result, your eating experience will be remarkable.

You may lighten your appetite with one of Restaurant Aura's many handmade soups or appetizers if seafood is too heavy for you. You won't find better dining options in Iceland than these spots.

Leaving your comfort zone behind is a great way to see the world. Therefore, don't be scared to eat in strange places. The experience will be enhanced by it.

**Things to Consider:**

Typical fare at the finest restaurants in Iceland, this woman is enjoying a little serving of fish and chips. Take these essential steps to maximize your Icelandic culinary experience before you even get off the aircraft. As a first step, try some different dishes. Something that seems weird could really be very tasty.

Consider the rich, delicious, and creamy Icelandic yogurt. Moreover, their lamb soup is just the thing to warm you up on chilly days. Though it may take some getting used to, you shouldn't totally dismiss hakari, or fermented shark.

Additionally, hang out with the natives. Join a social media group to find out about new places to eat or areas to explore. If you want to be a good budgeter, knowing the currency difference is a must.

Iceland is known for its high prices. Coming back from vacation shouldn't be a rude awakening, especially when it comes to prices. You will greatly enhance your gastronomic experience in Iceland if you bear these items in mind during your next visit.

EAT LIKE A LOCAL IN ICELAND: MUST-TRY FOODS

**Understanding Food in Iceland:**

Isolation and the severe northern temperatures had a profound impact on Icelandic cuisine, which is important to keep in mind while trying to make sense of Icelandic cuisine. The foundation of Icelandic cuisine is formed by robust root vegetables, wild berries, lamb, and fish. Long, cold winters have not stopped generations of Icelanders from preserving food using age-old techniques including smoking, drying, pickling, and fermenting.

Legend has it that courageous people in bygone days would prepare hákarl—a delicacy made by burning shark or lamb over sheep dung. However, Iceland's restaurant scene hasn't been static either. The culture of eating has changed throughout history, from the Viking Age through times of famine to the present day. These days, you can get Michelin-starred restaurants that provide creative takes on traditional dishes like cod cheeks and reindeer.

**Uncovering The Top Iceland Food Favorites:** Before you go on your journey to the country of fire and ice, make sure you savor the diverse array of flavors and textures found in Icelandic cuisine. Icelandic cuisine reflects the country's history and scenery via its delectable lamb meals, unusual fish specialties, distinctive dairy products, and delectable desserts.

**A list of the top traditional Icelandic foods you must sample to experience the true essence of this dramatic Nordic land.**

**Icelandic Hotdogs:**

Attention, frugal eaters! I present to you Icelandic Hotdogs. The Icelandic hot dog is the best affordable meal in Iceland, hands down. It has a flavor that no other cuisine can match. Put down those boring old hot dogs. With each mouthful, you'll get the ideal snap from the natural casings that contain a delectable combination of lamb, hog, and beef.

But it's the toppings that really make it special! The whole experience can be yours when you order "The Works," which includes a variety of mouth-watering toppings including fried and raw onions, sweet mustard, ketchup, remoulade sauce, mayonnaise, and relish.

Baejarins Beztu Pylsur serves the most genuine Icelandic hot dogs. Since 1937, this famous hot dog stand has been serving you these delicious treats. Prepare to have your taste senses blown away!

**Fish and Chips:** People who love fish and chips, take note! In your quest for the finest cuisine in Reykjavik, you must savor the legendary fish and chips. Almost every eatery in the city serves this mouth-watering specialty. The majority of Icelanders live near the water, and fishing is a big part of their economy, so you know you're getting seafood that is both fresh and delicious.

Fish such as cod, arctic char, halibut, haddock, and herring are among the more than 300 kinds of fish found in Icelandic waters. They provide a wide variety of delicious fish dishes, including sushi, stews, and the traditional fish and chips with a golden coating.

Kaffivagninn Restaurant on the ancient port has the best fish and chips in town. Established in 1935, this highly regarded jewel is one of the greatest restaurants in Reykjavik, promising diners an extraordinary culinary trip.

**Kjotsupa (Lamb Soup):**

The Reykjavik culinary scene is home to several delicious dishes, one of which being Kjotsupa (Lamb Soup). Tender lamb, root vegetables, rice, and aromatic herbs come together in harmony in this famous Icelandic stew, a mainstay in the country's cuisine.

The lamb, which is noted for its unique flavor from natural raising techniques, is grown locally and is the secret ingredient to its outstanding flavor. The unique Icelandic sheep are bred without the use of hormones or grain, making them an unforgettable treat.

Kaffi Loki, a typical home-style restaurant in downtown Reykjavik, is just across the street from Hallgrímskirkja church, so you may have true Kjotsupa. While in Iceland, make sure to try this delectable delicacy!

**Dried fish, or Harðfiskur:**

Are you prepared to savor the extraordinary tastes of Icelandic food? You should visit Harðfiskur because it provides an irresistible taste of authentic Icelandic cuisine.

This one-of-a-kind treat is made of dried fish, usually cod or haddock, which you can get in packages at almost every supermarket in the country. Envision the ideal snack: dry, crumbly, protein-rich fish jerky.

The dish is a must-try in Iceland, even if it's not a complete dinner. Add some delicious butter over top for a more genuine taste. Soak it up; no matter where you put it, the bag will release a lovely fishy aroma!

**Plokkfiskur (Fish Stew):**

Let us fill you in on one of Iceland's finest dishes, Plokkfiskur, the ultimate comfort food—fish stew. Plokkfiskur exemplifies the exceptional skill with which Icelanders, as an island country, prepare fresh, premium fish.

Imagine a delicious combination of milk, potatoes, and onions floating with delicate haddock or cod. Curry powder, cheese, or a delicious bechamel sauce are recent additions to certain versions.

In any case, the key is to keep things simple while piling on the flavor. Salka Valka has the recipe down pat, so if you want the tastiest Plokkfiskur, you should definitely stop by. Don't leave without trying their native Icelandic beer, too!

**Rúgbrauð (Rye Bread):**

Have you ever been curious about the flavor of a volcano? The closest thing you could find is Rúgbrauð, which is a kind of rye bread from Iceland.

What a brilliant use of geothermal heat to carefully bake this traditional Icelandic dish—it's sweet, rich, and delicious! The old method included locating a hot spring, placing a pot of dough in the ground, and allowing the earth's heat to rise the dough.

What was the outcome? This dense, almost cake-like bread is a mainstay in every Icelandic household. Do you want some? It is a staple on the menus of most American bakeries and restaurants.

**Humarsúpa (LobsterSoup):**

Humarsúpa, also known as lobster soup, should definitely be included in any "things to eat in Iceland" list. Humarsúpa, or Icelandic lobster soup, is a delicious food that brings together the savory langoustines, crunchy veggies, and velvety cream in a comforting stew.

As warm as a blanket on a cold Icelandic day, this soup is more than simply a meal. And what's even better? Enjoy this exquisite broth with a piece of freshly made bread! Húsið in Isafjordur is the spot to go if you want to sample this gastronomic marvel. All throughout the land and sea, its Humarsúpa is famous for its abundance of hefty langoustine chunks!

**Lambakjöt (Roasted Lamb):** Looking for some warm and comforting dishes to satisfy your hunger while in Iceland? Greetings, Lambakjöt! For good reason, lamb is an essential part of Icelandic cuisine. Icelandic sheep produce very thin, succulent meat because they graze on wild, verdant plants and berries.

Icelandic lamb, known as lambakjöt, is a hearty dish that you should not miss. It is often roasted with herbs from the area and served with root vegetables and sauce. Visit Við Pollinn Restaurant in Isafjordur while you're in the breathtaking Westfjords.

A juicy, fall-off-the-bone Lambakjöt is just one of the buffet-style dishes that have made this quaint, rustic restaurant famous. When paired with the breathtaking views of the fjord, this restaurant will make you want more than just the food!

**Lightly Salted Cod:**

The simple but exquisite mildly salted fish is one of the greatest foods to eat in Iceland. Be not deceived, however it may seem easy!

Light salting brings out the sweetness and delicate taste of the fish caught in Iceland, straight from the cold North Atlantic. The usual next step is to pan-sear it until it's brown, which seals in all the liquids and makes for the most delicious crunch and flaky inside.

Where can one most savor this delicacy? A traditional restaurant, pizza, and bar in Hólmavík is Café Riis. Café Riis, located in this picturesque fishing hamlet, is a must-visit for every Icelandic gourmet since it provides the best salted cod on the island.

**Pan-Seared Rainbow Trout:**

Looking for the top Icelandic dishes? Try pan-seared rainbow trout. Pan-Seared Rainbow Trout is a delectable treat that we hope you'll try. They have perfected the skill of making this fantastic meal at Restaurant Dunhagi in Tálknafjörður.

Imagine delicate rainbow trout, flaky and delicate within, with a perfectly crispy outside that will make your taste buds dance. With a blend of fjord-fresh herbs and spices, this meal captures the essence of Iceland's pure waters.

Not to mention the welcoming atmosphere of one of the fjord's oldest structures. Try this restaurant speciality at Restaurant Dunhagi for a once-in-a-lifetime taste of Icelandic cuisine!

**Skyr:** Skyr is a centuries-old curd cheese that tastes like yogurt and is a favorite Icelandic dish. But it has lately become quite popular with both residents and visitors.

It has a creamy, somewhat sour flavor that comes from combining skim milk with microorganisms. Plain or with honey and fruit was the traditional way to consume Skyr. These days, this popular Icelandic dessert comes in a wide variety of flavors, including passion fruit and coconut-chocolate-banana!

Be sure to sample Strikin's Skyr while you're in Akureyri; they take a traditional dessert and make it into something so good it almost melts in your lips.

**Rjúpa (Rock Ptarmigan):**

Rjúpa, also known as Rock Ptarmigan, is the dish that best represents the untamed nature of the Icelandic highlands. The delicate, somewhat gamey flesh of this game bird has a distinctive taste profile, making it a popular delicacy, particularly around Christmas.

Roasting the chicken with Icelandic herbs and spices or braising it in a robust stew are two common preparations. The subtle flavors of the bird are brought out by these preparation techniques, which are a true reflection of its natural environment.

In addition to revealing Iceland's culinary heritage, rjúpa reveals the country's reverence for its natural surroundings. For any gourmet exploring North Iceland, it is an absolute must-try.

**Hangikjöt (Smoked Lamb):**

Now, let's discuss Hangikjöt, a traditional Icelandic delicacy that is sure to please any gourmet. Smoked lamb, or hangikjöt, isn't the usual fare for meat lovers.

To get its distinctive flavor, the lamb is slowly smoked over birchwood or dried sheep dung, making it taste like a delectable culinary souvenir from Iceland. The end product is a smokey, juicy treat that will have you begging for more.

Are you prepared to go on a culinary journey? Hver Restaurant in Reykjavik is a must-visit. They might easily use their Hangikjöt as a symbol of Iceland's world-renowned cuisine. You should not miss this feast, especially when served with classic rye bread or creamy potato mash.

**Salsa de Lifrarpylsa:**

Lifrarpylsa, or liver sausage in English, is a common dish in Iceland that you may want to try if you're curious in the local cuisine. The name shouldn't deter you, however.

Traditional Icelandic comfort food, this specialty is produced with a mixture of rye flour, sheep's liver, suet, and a casing. What was the outcome? The natives rave about this flavorful sausage because of its richness and heartiness.

It is often smeared on toast or served cooked with potatoes and turnips. You won't want to miss out on this one-of-a-kind experience since Lifrarpylsa is available in almost every Icelandic store!

**Gravlax:**

Is Gravlax something you're familiar with? If you haven't been to Vik, Iceland, yet, allow us to introduce you to some of the greatest food in the world—and one of the best examples of Nordic cuisine. Fresh salmon is traditionally cured with salt, sugar, and dill to make gravlax. Seems easy, doesn't it? However, the flavor is really revolting. The salmon takes on a lovely, subtle flavor as it cures, making it a delicate treat that will captivate your taste buds from the very first mouthful. To satisfy your seafood cravings, consider Gravlax, which is usually served thinly sliced on rye toast or with boiled potatoes.

**Kleina:** Kleina, one of Icelandic cuisine's crown jewels, is about to be served, so get ready pastry lovers. Envision a crispy, sugar-dusted, elegantly twisted dough pastry infused with a hint of cardamom.
Imagine that! It's really amazing! Indeed, that is the case! When we say that Kleina and doughnuts are a match made in confectionary heaven, we mean it in the most literal sense. A little crunch on the outside and fluffy, soft interior will have you begging for more.

The greatest thing is that you can find Kleina at almost every Icelandic coffee establishment. On a cold Icelandic morning, it goes well with coffee, and in the afternoon, it's a delightful sweet treat.

**Rúllupylsa (Rolled Sausage):**

Let us present you to Rúllupylsa, a dish that is often considered to be among the finest in Iceland. You can obtain this traditional Icelandic Christmas treat—rolled sausage—anytime of year, which is a relief.

A thick chunk of lamb rib is encased in a flavorful mixture of spices and herbs. Imagine a satisfying combination of umami and festive spirit. After that, it's time to let the sausage cure so you may enjoy it cold, cut thinly on toast.

You may be wondering, "Where can I get this delicious dish?" In Iceland, Rúllupylsa is available at the majority of supermarkets and butcher shops. Be sure to pick up some Rúllupylsa, a snack that is authentically Icelandic, as you are preparing for your road trip around the country.

**Pönnukökur (Icelandic Pancakes):**

Icelandic pancakes, or Pönnukökur, are a must-try for dessert lovers visiting Iceland. Pönnukökur is thinner and more like French crêpes than pancakes made in the American way. They are fried to a beautiful brown on a specialized griddle using a batter that consists of eggs, flour, sugar, and milk. Deliciously soft with a little crunch around the edges, that is the finished result. Enjoyed anytime of day, they are usually filled with sugar or fruit jam and served wrapped up. But where can you get the Pönnukökur that you've been craving?

You may find these sweets in many Icelandic households, but you can also get them at cafes, bakeries, and even festival street food stands.

## THE 10 BEST ICELAND CLUBS & BARS

At night, Reykjavik comes to life. Weekends see some clubs staying open until 5:30 in the morning, with dance floors packed until the last dancers leave. But if you want to relax in a booth with a cold beer, there are several excellent microbars that serve beers made in the area.

Here are thirteen of Reykjavik's most famous nightclubs and pubs, broken down for your perusal. Whether you're in the mood for a live jazz venue or a spectacular drag performance, Iceland is sure to have something to offer your next vacation.

**Kaldi Bar:** On Laugavegur street, you'll find the charming Kaldi Bar. This is Reykjavik's major retail street, and there are a lot of other pubs on the corner that you may visit at the same time. You may sample a wide variety of regional gins and specialty beers, and there's a piano for those special occasions when you want to hear some live music. There are many of comfortable spots to settle into and have a nice catch-up with pals, and the atmosphere is casual and welcoming.

The service at the Kaldi bar is very well-liked. Friendly and well-informed, the bartenders will do whatever to make you feel comfortable. Our closing hour on weekends is about 3 in the morning. Even though Kaldi closes at around 1 am on Sundays and Mondays, the bar is still open throughout the weekend.

**Skuli Craft Bar:** Another place to unwind in style is Skuli Craft Bar. Unless you are already aware of its existence, you probably wouldn't be able to discover it because of how hidden away it is on Aðalstraeti.

With fourteen constantly changing beer taps, patrons may sample more than one hundred thirty varieties of high-quality, regional brews. You may expect to encounter some welcoming locals at this pub as it is not located in a very touristic neighborhood.

You have the option to either order meals to go or dine from the food truck parked in the outside area. That this pub is peaceful and off the beaten path is something that many people appreciate. There are those who think it's a little too laid-back and would rather be on the livelier Laugavegur street.

Saturdays and Sundays at 1 am, and 11 pm, Sunday through Thursday, is when Skuli shuts.

**Bravó:** There is a wonderful mix of residents and visitors at Bravó, a pub and restaurant with fantastic community atmosphere. Located on Laugavegur, you may usually hear live music, so be sure to check the schedule for any upcoming concerts while you're there.

It seems like every time you turn around, someone is dancing on the little dance floor! However, it's more of a pub than a nightclub, with plenty of intimate seating for socializing. Those who dress and appear differently than the norm are warmly welcomed, and the place becomes rather full during happy hour. (Conversely, there is no specific clothing code that will guarantee you a warm welcome.)

If you're longing for the company of a furry friend, Bravó is a great place to see neighborhood dogs! Not only that, but the pizzas are delicious and the beer prices are fair.

**Microbar Reykjavik:** One other welcoming watering hole in Reykjavik that serves high-quality beers from the area is Microbar. Do you see a pattern here? We suggest a pub crawl if you're in the mood for a wild night out since Reykjavik is teeming with little pubs serving artisan beer.

Caution is advised! Due to their inability to get a lease extension, Reykjavik Microbar is now closed. While you're in town, be sure to check their official website to see whether they're up and running in their new location in the city.

The fact that it received some of Iceland's most rave reviews for local beer—and that many locals can't wait for it to reopen—makes it worthy of inclusion on our list.

**Gamli Gaukurinn:** Everyone, regardless of their gender or sexual orientation, is welcome at Gamli Gaukurinn. "We welcome everyone, except for assholes," they said themselves. Racism, sexism, and homophobia are not tolerated under any circumstances. In addition to being the first legal draft beer served following prohibition, the restrooms are gender-neutral. You can see live music performances on a monthly basis, as well as drag shows and karaoke. This is the perfect spot for you if you want to relax and be yourself among kind people. Vegan options abound, and the bartenders are quick and kind to boot. At happy hour, prices are rock bottom.

Tryggvagta is where you'll discover this magical spot. On weekends, it shuts at 3 in the morning, while on weekdays, it closes at 1 in the morning.

**Pablo Discobar:** Among the most well-known clubs in Reykjavik, Pablo Discobar is a great place to go dancing. We have the perfect place for you if you like a riot of color and a collection of unusual furnishings. Drink a margarita while dancing to '70s music at this spot that's "so tacky that it's chic," as several regulars put it.

The clothing code is technically smart-casual, but the bouncers aren't always consistent in letting people in based on that rule. Therefore, it is prudent not to wear sneakers just in case. The club has a policy of no patrons older than 25 on weekends.
On weekends and holidays, Pablo Discobar shuts at 3 in the morning, while on weekdays, it closes at 1 in the morning. This is located on Veltusund.

Near the harbor in Reykjavik, you'll find the very entertaining Smokin Puffin. If I had to guess, I'd say the owner is the most beloved aspect of this establishment by everybody. With a cold one in hand, you and your pals may take refuge from the storm outside as you play darts or table football. Even if you aren't in the company of pals, the warm hospitality will more than compensate.
You shouldn't think twice about getting the Choco Puffin drink while you're here since everyone loves it. The usual hours of operation are from 10:00 am to 10:00 pm.

**The Secret Cellar:** If you'd rather not dance the night away, you can always see a comedy performance at The Secret Cellar. In all of Reykjavik, there is only one comedy club. Every night, at about 8 o'clock, there is an English-speaking entertainment, and then there is karaoke.

All the tourists agree: it's a great spot to go for a night of fun and laughter. The performances, however, aren't always up to par because of the venue's diminutive size. Until you arrive, you have no idea what to anticipate; thus, you should just relax and consume an abundance of beer.

**Húrra:** Húrra is a pub and music venue close to the harbor. It's also the name of a clothes shop in the area, so double-check that you're going in the correct direction.

Jazz concerts are held on Mondays, while on weekends, DJs spin the tunes. Local musicians often perform there throughout the week, so make sure to keep an eye on their activities. Happy hour lasts until 10 p.m., and the prices are really affordable considering they are in Reykjavik. There will be a lot of locals there, so be ready to dance the night away!

Fridays and Saturdays see the venue open until 4:30 am, while other days see it shut at 1 am.

**Dillon Whiskey Bar:** In the chilly Icelandic winters, a fine whiskey might be a welcome companion at Dillon Whiskey Bar. If you're feeling overwhelmed by the selection of more than 150 whiskies offered at Dillon Whiskey Bar, don't worry—the bartenders are happy to assist you in making your selection. Since their whiskey drinks might get pricey during peak hours, we advise you to check out their happy hour.

On weekends, this pub is very busy—and occasionally rowdy—due to its free live music events. Therefore, this may be an excellent option if you are seeking a buzz. On the other hand, if you'd rather have a more laid-back conversation with your pals in a pub like Smokin Puffin or Kaldi, you could be better served.

Situated on Laugavegur, Dillon Whiskey Bar usually shuts at around 1 in the morning.

**Kaffibarin:** When the sun goes down, Kaffibarin transforms into a dance club. On weekends, you may expect a fairly large crowd, considering its little size. Although the bartenders have been receiving some fairly nasty reviews as of late, the DJs are known to be excellent at interpreting the energy in the room. Smokin' Puffin is the place to go if you're seeking very pleasant service, since the proprietor, a bearded gentleman, is said in almost every review to be both courteous and welcoming.

Kaffibarin is worth a visit if you're not picky about the friendliness of the service and would rather listen to excellent music. To ensure the privacy of all guests, Kaffibarin asks that no pictures be taken within the venue. Despite the fact that this is a welcome change from the digital realm, you may be requested to put down your camera. Given its long history, it's hardly surprising that they adhere to certain traditional practices.

**Kiki Queer Bar:** Despite its little size, Kiki Queer Bar manages to draw a respectable clientele. Gay folks seeking sanctuary may find greater options at Gamli Gaukurinn. Despite its largely positive evaluations, Kiki may get overrun with visitors seeking a good time and lacks an entirely welcoming atmosphere. During the busiest times of year, you probably won't run across many gay residents. However, you can be very content here if you're seeking to meet other travelers. Popular options include drag performances and karaoke.

As the sun goes down, you'll hear everyone dancing and singing. You should definitely give it a go if you're ok with cramming up close to random people as you dance the night away.

**The Irishman Pub:** Although it is one of Reykjavik's more recent establishments, The Irishman Pub has quickly gained a stellar reputation for its welcoming ambiance and, on most days, unexpectedly lengthy happy hours, which run from 12 noon until 7 pm. Guests may enjoy live music on a regular basis, and there's a private Karaoke room available for parties. Enjoy a pint of Guinness in the booths adorned with lovely oak furnishings on a cozy evening.

# CHAPTER EIGHT
## BEST ICELAND BEACHES TO VISIT RIGHT NOW

The beaches of Iceland are breathtaking and unlike any other. The island, which is about the size of Kentucky, is ringed by an 828-mile ring road. This allows you to reach many of Iceland's remote beaches, where you may enjoy the crisp air rather than soaking up the sun.

All of Iceland's top beaches, whether they're long stretches of golden sand or narrow black-sand strips, have a similar trait: they all provide breathtaking views of the untamed ocean.

Expect nothing less than the best when you visit the beaches of Iceland, whether it's on a day trip from Reykjavík or you're exploring the northern fjord districts.

**Djúpalónssandur Beach:**

This sand and stone beach, which is part of the curving volcanic landscape on the western coast of Iceland, clings to the Snaefellsnes Peninsula.

Follow the trail that branches off the highway and goes through a lava field with sharp lava structures to get to Djúpalónssandur.

The 8,000-year-old lava tube known as Vatnshellir Cave was formed during a volcanic eruption that altered the terrain; see it before you go to the beach. Entering the 114-foot cave via a spiral stairway, guides provide interesting tours of Vatnshellir.

The English trawler Epine GY 7, which went down in 1948, has her shell on the beach for everybody to see. The loss of life was 14 tragically.

The fishing settlements of Hellnar and Arnarstapi, as well as the towering cliffs of Lóndrangar, are among the breathtaking coastline observation locations that should be visited when approaching Djúpalónssandur.

Wear clothes as you explore the shoreline of Iceland; you never know whether you could be greeted by a balmy summer day or by the untamed west with its rolling mist, wind, and rain.

**Ytri-Tunga Beach:**

On the Snæfellsnes Peninsula, two hours north of Reykjavík along the rugged coastline of Iceland, is the stunning Ytri-Tunga Beach, where you may swim in the crystal-clear waters.

Dreamy Ytri-Tunga stands out with its golden coastline, whereas other Icelandic beaches have black sand.

In the summer, visitors to the area may be treated to the sight of harbor seals or gray seals resting on the rocks along the coast. Remember to maintain a safe distance—approximately 165 feet—and bring your camera to photograph these stunning underwater animals.

**Ólafsfjörður Beach, near Akureyri:**

Ólafsfjörður, a magnificent black-sand beach on Iceland's northern shore, is situated at the entrance of the Eyjafjörður fjord and is encircled by snow-capped mountains. As the snow from the winter melts away, it becomes cascading waterfalls all around Iceland during the summer.

The beach looks out over the fishing hamlet of Ólafsfjörður, which is flanked by the trout-filled Ólafsfjörður lake and is lined with colorful wood buildings.

Go for a stroll down the beach and take in the breathtaking views. This expansive beach has an air of total seclusion. You could discover the beach all to yourself, despite the fact that the little town is just a fifteen-minute stroll away.

**Reynisfjara Beach:**

It is well worth the two and a half hour drive from Reykjavik to see the breathtaking Reynisfjara Beach on the south coast.

With its dramatic black coastlines, crashing Atlantic waves, and jagged rock formations, Reynisfjara is among Iceland's top beaches.

Reynisfjara isn't the best beach on the island for swimming or bathing, but that doesn't mean you can't have fun here.

Grab a coffee from the beachside Black Beach Restaurant and stroll a short distance to the shoreside Hálsanefshellir Cave. Soaring basalt columns form the ceiling of the breathtaking sea cave Hálsanefshellir, which lies at the foot of Reynisfjall mountain on the most eastern point of Reynisfjara.

Stop by Vik í Myrdal, the most southernmost settlement on mainland Iceland, when you're visiting Reynisfjara. It's like stepping into a fairytale.
From atop a hill stands a charming white church, and all around it are cafes and restaurants, such as a pizza, a place to try craft beers, and the posh Icelandic spot, Berg.

**Dyrholaey Beach:**
Located west of Reynisfjara, Dyrholaey Beach is one of the top beaches in Iceland. It stretches for kilometers along the south coast, which is mostly undeveloped.
Located on Dyrhólaey, often called the Endless Black Beach, is the white-cubed Dyrhólaeyjarviti lighthouse, which serves to alert ships in the harbor to the serrated rocks offshore.
The spectacular arch formed by coastal erosion is the most recognizable feature of this volcanic beach. In 1993, a pilot made headlines when famously piloting a tiny aircraft through its massive size. Nature enthusiasts will be enchanted by Dyrhólaey since it is a haven for migrating Atlantic puffins from May to September and eider ducks all year round.
Skógafoss, a rumbling Icelandic waterfall with a plunge of around 200 feet, is not far distant and should be seen.

**Búðir Beach:**

Located on the border of the expansive Búðahraun lava field in west Iceland, Búðir Beach is a long stretch of golden sand that faces Faxaflói Bay.

This area was formed around 5,000 to 8,000 years ago when lava spilled from the core crater of the Búðaklettur volcano.

Since 1977, the beach has had the status of a natural reserve. During the summer, you may stroll amid the stunning fields of wildflowers that flourish here. In addition, tourists have the option to explore Búðahellir, a cavern that extends 1,253 feet into the crater.

Soak up some rays while strolling around the beach. The shoreline is littered with black lava rocks, which provide as a constant reminder of the dynamic geology of Iceland.

Admire the picturesque Búðakirkja, a jet-black church constructed in the 19th century, situated next to the seashore, as well as the adjacent horsetail-shaped Bjarnarfoss. From the road behind the beach, one can watch the water falling. Stop at the vantage point above the waterfall if you have some free time.

**Álftanes Beach, near Reykjavik:**

Just twenty minutes south of Reykjavik, on the dynamic Reykjanes peninsula, is one of the nearest beaches to Iceland's capital, Álftanes.

Nestled among verdant fields, Álftanes is in close proximity to two notable landmarks: Bessastaðir, the official house of the President of Iceland, and Bessastaðakirkja, a beautiful white church.

Both lovely and historically significant, Bessastaðir is a real find. Since the 1940s, the farmhouse that was formerly owned by Snorri Sturluson—a renowned scholar from Iceland and the King of Norway after Sturluson's murder—has served as the seat of Icelandic democracy.

Grab a cup of coffee at the quaint Álftanes café in town, where you can also find mouthwatering handmade soups, luscious sourdough breads, and decadent pastries.

With several routes crisscrossing the headland, Álftanes Beach is ideal for hikers. Begin your climb with a scramble around Gálgahraun, a huge lava field where, according to excavations, executions probably occurred at the time when Iceland was a colony (around 870-930).

**Nautholsvik Beach, Reykjavik:**

Nautholsvik is one of the top beaches in Iceland due to its convenient location and the chance it gives guests to dive into the cool sea.

Despite their stunning beauty, few of Iceland's beaches are really swimmable. As a result of a sea wall that was constructed in 2001, Nauthólsvík stands out as an anomaly. The lagoon it forms is filled with hot water that is poured into the pool, resulting in summertime temperatures ranging from 15°-19°C (59°-66°F).

Relax on the crescent coastline while swimming casually. In addition to showers, changing rooms, hot tubs, and steam baths, there are also restrooms.

**Langisandur Beach, near Reykjavik:**

Located about half an hour north of Reykjavik, this sandy beach on the west coast of Iceland has been awarded the Blue Flag.

The drive here is breathtaking, with the roadway winding its way between towering mountains and seemingly unending ocean views.

Get your swimwear or hiking pants zipped up and get ready to splash about in the water. Joining locals and knowledgeable tourists in Guðlaug Baths, located just beyond Langisandur Beach, for a relaxing hot bath is one of the top things to do on the beach.

The Akranes Folk Museum is a charming place to visit if you have some free time. Through audio narrative, artifacts, and pictures, the museum chronicles the history of this area of Iceland's western shore, spanning from the 17th century to the current day.

**Solheimasandur Beach:**

Located on the southern coast of Iceland, Solheimasandur Beach is well-known for both its black sand and the aircraft disaster that occurred there in 1973. Fortunately, everyone on board the DC aircraft belonging to the United States Navy made it out alive.

Close inspection of the eerie debris on Solheimasandur Beach produces for breathtaking photography.

A magnificent flowing waterfall in Iceland, Sólheimasandur is only a short drive away. Come here after you've had your fill of Solheimasandur Beach to wander behind the 200-foot water curtain.

Located within a tight canyon, Gljufrabui is another stunning waterfall that is easily accessible on foot from Seljalandsfoss.

**Meleyri Beach, near Seydisfjordur**

Faraway Meleyri Beach on the east coast of Iceland is typical of the country's beaches—pristine shorelines with few, if any, facilities—and is located close to Seydisfjordur.

The volcanic sand beach in Breiðdalsvík borders the ring road of Iceland, making it relatively simple to visit despite its remote location.

The stunning Eastfjords, a 75-mile stretch in the northeast of the nation, with its sharp cliffs, tiny fjords, and charming fishing communities, are a part of the route that passengers follow from Seydisfjordur.

Hiking and appreciating Iceland's nature is made ideal in Meleyri. The region's wild reindeer may be out and about, so keep an eye out.

After a satisfying beach trek, craft beer enthusiasts can visit the little town of Breiðdalsvík to Beljandi Brewery to try some local ales.

**Hofsós Beach, near Akureyri:**

One of the most northern beaches in Iceland, Hofsós is located close to Akureyri and stretches along a narrow stretch of the smooth Skagafjörður fjord. It lies at 65 degrees north latitude. The little, volcanic Hofsós Beach is bordered by an ascending grassy bank.

Take a two-minute stroll from the beach to the basalt columns of Staðarbjörg, following the roadside stairs down to the coast, to enjoy peaceful views of the fjord.

Despite its size, the colorful fishing hamlet of Hofsós has a museum, grocery shop, public pool, and restaurant in addition to its many other amenities.

Take a look at the exhibit at the exodus Center that details the 18th-century exodus of Icelanders to the Americas.

Hofsós Beach wouldn't be complete without a visit to Grafarkirkja, Iceland's oldest turf church and a place straight out of a fairy tale. The current church building is from the 17th century, while this site has a history of previous churches.

The interior of Grafarkirkja is off-limits to the public, but the grounds, which include a tiny cemetery protected by a circular turf wall, are available to exploration.

**Rauðisandur Beach:**

Reached in less than 2.5 hours from Ísafjörður in the Westfjords, Rauðisandur Beach is one of the most stunning beaches in Iceland. Its moniker, Red Sands, is due to its velvety, ochre-tinged coastline.

It is an expedition to reach Rauðisandur. Along with the journey, guests will also have to conquer a little trek starting from the parking area.

Witness the incredible summer turnout of birdwatchers from all around the globe at Rauðisandur, which is located on the same coastline as Látrabjarg, the highest cliffs in Europe.

Keep an eye out for guillemots, puffins, razorbills, and gulls as you gaze out to the ocean and the ashy rocks that encircle Rauðisandur.

You may see seals lounging on the beach or in the water all the time. With a close gaze, you could even get a glimpse of dolphins soaring over the waves or humpback whales smacking their tails.

**Þingeyri Beach, near Ísafjörður:**

The picturesque Dýrafjörður fjord and the exciting Westfjords Alps outline the little village of Þingeyri. Another black-sand beach in Iceland is located there as well.

Stop into Simbahöllin, the village café, for some comforting hot beverages and Belgian waffles before you go down to the beach. You may rent bikes at Simbahöllin and explore Þingeyri and its relaxing beach on your own. The owners also provide horseback riding courses.

Exciting sea kayak tours that leave from the beach are a must-do for water sports enthusiasts. With the help of a knowledgeable local guide, row into the glistening 20-mile-long fjord in search of seals basking on the rocks.

Bring a waterproof cover for your camera since there are many chances to shoot animals, such as migrating birds, seals, and humpback whales in the summer.

**Sandvik Beach, near Reykjavik:**

Located on the breathtaking Reykjanes peninsula that juts out into the North Atlantic Ocean, this stunning black beach is adjacent to Iceland's Blue Lagoon geothermal resort.
Sandvik is a sloping beach nestled in the middle of the expansive volcanic terrain of the area, and there are many opportunities for peaceful Icelandic treks.
You may take pleasure in a brisk ankle-deep paddle even if the waves are too high to swim.
Keep an eye out for the remains of a ship that went down this spot in 1981 while the tide is out.

You may next make a pit break at the adjacent Bridge Between Continents to walk over the iconic footbridge that spans a wide rift that separates the North American and Eurasian tectonic plates. The beaches of Iceland are just as breathtaking as the country's icy fjords, azure glaciers, and raging volcanoes. Discover the enchanted region of Iceland on a luxurious cruise with Celebrity Cruises.

# ROMANTIC PLACES IN ICELAND: SPOTS TO WOO YOUR PARTNERS!

Iceland is a popular honeymoon vacation due to its stunning surroundings, which include picturesque settlements, verdant farms, beautiful beaches, hot spas, stunning glacier vistas, the northern lights, and more. Organizing a vacation to Iceland might be a daunting task. Here are some must-see locations for your honeymoon in Iceland to kick off your preparations.

**Top Icelandic Spots for a Honeymoon**

**Jokulsarlon Glacier Lagoon:**

One of the must-see attractions in Iceland is Jokulsarlon Glacier Lagoon, widely regarded as one of the world's most picturesque locations. Vatnajokull National Park, a World Heritage Site recognized by UNESCO, is home to this breathtaking glacier lake. Jokulsarlon has also been a favorite setting for films in Hollywood, Bollywood, and Game of Thrones.

One of Iceland's deepest lakes, Jokulsarlon supposedly had its ice glaciers produced a thousand years ago. As it is now, Jokulsarlon is a year-round vacation spot. During the summer, boat trips on the lagoon are available, providing an excellent opportunity to see the icebergs up close. At the lake's mouth, seals congregate in winter, providing a picture-perfect setting for nature photographers and wildlife watchers.

It becomes rather busy throughout the day, so if you want to avoid the crowds, we recommend getting there early—preferably before dawn. Near the lake, you'll find a large parking lot with restrooms. These icebergs melt and drift to Diamond Beach, where they eventually join the open sea, which is just a short walk away.

**Diamond Beach:**

Diamond Beach, formerly known as Jokulsarlon Beach, is a picturesque spot ideal for honeymoon photos in the southern section of Iceland's Ring Road. Pieces of glacier from neighboring icebergs wash up on the coast as the tide rolls in. Excited newlyweds can't wait to find the beached diamond-ice shards that sparkle on the volcanic black sand. Gather a few of these diamonds, give them as gifts, and pose for a couple's selfie next to the glacier chunks of varying sizes. Is there anything more enchanting than seeing the dawn or dusk in this breathtaking scenery?

Diamond Beach does not have any lodging options. Just a short drive away in Vik or Hofn are a few of hotels. A trip to Diamond Beach, whether during the day or at night to see the northern lights, is still possible from either of these two little settlements.

**BlueLagoon:**

Picture yourself and your loved one floating on a bed of lovely, steaming milky water in a blue lagoon, surrounded by ice and with the steam from the water making it hard to see anything beyond the surface. You're looking at Blue Lagoon! The majority of tourists learn about Iceland via pictures of Blue Lagoon or the Northern Lights, making it one of the most recognizable landmarks in the country. Blue Lagoon should be your first stop on your honeymoon to Iceland. To prevent crowds, it is essential to arrange your visit at the official Blue Lagoon website as early as possible and select the beginning of the day. Everything you need is to show up to this cutting-edge facility and have a good time.

Schedule an underwater massage if you want to sink into a state of profound relaxation. Floating on calm geothermal waters is a fascinating and relaxing way to experience nature's heat. Indulge in a clay mask for radiant skin and smooth it with cleaning oil. Be careful to stay hydrated since the typical individual spends three to five hours here, which may not seem like much. If you and your loved one are looking for a romantic getaway, Blue Lagoon is the perfect place to unwind and celebrate this wonderful occasion.

**Snaefellsnes Peninsula:**

Incredible waterfalls, cliffs, glaciers, hotsprings, picturesque settlements, lava fields, beaches with black and golden sand, and much more can be found on the Snaefellsnes Peninsula. All the best of Iceland, in a nutshell, is right there. The Snaefellsnes Peninsula is easily accessible from Reykjavik, so it's perfect for day trips or longer stays. Even if you're only in Iceland for a short period of time, you really must see this stunning location. An equally wonderful and less congested alternative for the world-famous Golden Circle trip in Iceland is the Snaefellsnes Peninsula. It is a favorite spot for newlyweds in Iceland because of its seclusion.

**Reykjavik:**

The capital city of Iceland, Reykjavik, is a fantastic location for a honeymoon. If you're looking for a romantic getaway with lots of activities, this is the perfect spot for you. As an example, the Harpa Reykjavik Concert Hall is the perfect place for a romantic evening out. Countless great musical performances are very delightful. Seeing the Northern Lights is another romantic activity in Reykjavik. No trip to Reykjavik is complete without taking in this natural wonder with your significant other. In the vicinity of Reykjavik, Grótta is the ideal spot for this. If you are looking for a spot to go on a romantic stroll among scenic nature, this is a wonderful choice.

Reykjavik offers a variety of venues perfect for a romantic evening. Take the Reykjavik Domes as an example; they're fantastic. A few kilometers outside of Reykjavik, it provides a magnificent tent with all the amenities you might want for a romantic getaway. However, there are also numerous charming hotels in the heart of the city. Furthermore, Reykjavik offers a plethora of enjoyable activities.

**Skogafoss:**

Standing before a waterfall while kissing your sweetheart is the most romantic thing ever. An iconic romance moment that was included in Thor: The Dark World and Vikings must be considered among the best of all time. The one thing that makes Skogafoss a perfect "10" is picturing yourself and your beloved swooping down from the sky on dragons to steal a holy kiss, much like Daenerys Targaryen and Jon Snow from Game of Thrones.

Unspoiled beauty and romance await you at Skogafoss, where "foss" means "waterfall" in Icelandic. With a width of 82 feet (25 meters) and a plunge of 200 feet (60 meters), Skogafoss is one of the biggest waterfalls in Iceland. On bright days, the waterfall's continual backspray helps generate some stunning single and double rainbows. It goes without saying that this adds an extra dose of magic to this unique spot. A path starting from the eastern side of the waterfall and ascending to the pass of Fimmvorðuhals between the Eyjafjallajokull and Myrdalsjoku glaciers is perfect for active couples who want to go hiking or trekking.

**Fjadrargljufur Canyon:** One of the most enchanted places in Iceland to go on a honeymoon is the breathtaking Fjadrargljufur Canyon.

The massive canyon, which can be found in southern Iceland, is approximately 2 kilometers long and 100 meters deep. Its narrow, serpentine profile and steep canyon walls set it apart. The lovely trail that follows the canyon's edge is perfect for adventurers and hikers who want to spend quality time together. Amazing vistas of the canyon below, the rocks all around, and even a waterfall or two will be your reward.

Due to the low water level, you may even stroll down the canyon bottom. Since you'll have to wade in some sections, dress for the weather—cold and wet. In any case, you're going to like this breathtaking spot with its mossy paths, breathtaking blue waterways, and breathtaking vistas. Make the most of it by bringing a picnic for two to savor as you go.

It will take around three and a half hours to travel the 255 kilometers from Reykjavik, the capital, to the canyon. Kirkjubaejarklaustur is a great place to stay; it's just a 20-minute drive away. A variety of comfortable lodging alternatives are available in the little town.

**Hornafjordur:**

Despite its youth as a tourist destination, Hornafjordur is right up there with the best of them thanks to its abundance of exciting activities. For example, hornafjordur's enchantment will remain unmatched by the excitement of Pheonix or any other tourist attraction. It is an ideal honeymoon spot in Iceland since it is a whole another planet.

The national park of Vatnajokull was formed by the natural fusion of glacial ice, rivers, and a volcano, so it's a good place to start. Glacial World also has geothermal spas where you and your partner may relax while taking in the stunning alpine scenery. Additionally, you have the option to stay in houses.

Hofn Eagle Air offers guests aerial excursions, so they may observe things from a bird's-eye view. I think we can all agree that this is going to be a fantastic honeymoon. The boat trip of Jokulsarlon's glacier lagoon is something you must do. You may go sightseeing, take pictures, and spend quality time with your significant other.

**Djupavogskorin Geothermal Pool:**

If you're looking for a romantic way to spend an hour or two in Iceland, you should definitely check out the Djupavogskorin Geothermal Pool. Located in the far east of Iceland, halfway between Hofn and Djupivogur, lies a unique and secret hot spring. A tiny parking area with a boiling hot spring is located just off Road 1. Cotton grass and harebells around the spring in the summer, while snow covers the land in the winter. Hideaway hot tub access is via a boardwalk and a narrow trail that winds around a hill. Here is the hot tub and a laundry stand; otherwise, there is nothing. But the breathtaking views of the Atlantic Ocean from this heated pool are available all year.

On a honeymoon to Iceland, this free and compact hot tub would be perfect for a relaxing bath. Nothing beats a relaxing dip in the snow or beneath the twinkling northern lights, and you'll probably have the place to yourself.

**Hveragerdi Thermal River:**

On the honey moon, you may want to spend some time at Hveragerdi Thermal River, one of Iceland's most popular natural hot springs. You may easily visit the hot springs as a day trip from Reykjavík since they are only 40 minutes away. It is a three-kilometer trek from the settlement of Hveragerdi to that location. The trek is not only simple, but also quite scenic. Hot thermal ponds dot the countryside surrounding Hveragerdi, which also offers a glimpse of a nearby waterfall.

If you want to take it to the next level, you may inquire with local horse farms about tours that include riding to the hot springs. The hot springs are also great in the fall, when it's cool enough to jump in as the sun goes down. The thermal river is a good place to try to get a glimpse of the northern lights.

Hveragerdi is a great place for a honeymoon since, despite its beauty, it is not a very popular destination. As a result, you won't have to worry about being overrun by other tourists. That way you may bask in the soft, romantic light.

## ROMANTIC THINGS TO DO IN ICELAND

Here you can find all the information you need to make your next vacation more romantic! Here we will go over the top 12 things to do in Iceland for a romantic weekend. Every couple visiting the country of fire and ice may find something special among our breathtaking natural treasures, fascinating adventures, snug getaways, and unique experiences!

**Take in the northern lights:**

Between the months of October and March, a romantic getaway to Iceland is certain to provide you and your loved one with an unforgettable experience. The Northern Lights, or Aurora Borealis, are awe-inspiring, so settle down and marvel at them. As the sky fills with glistening green and purple streaks, you may relax in happiness.

Renting a camper van for your Icelandic vacation allows you to park wherever the scenery inspires you and snuggle up under the lights, so you can enjoy the northern lights in all their natural glory.

**Blue lagoon:**

This geothermal spa, located on the Reykjanes Peninsula in southwest Iceland, is ideal for couples who hire cars in Iceland for a romantic day trip. It is only fifteen minutes from Keflavík International Airport and thirty minutes from Reykjavik, the capital. The spa, restaurant, and café on site make it the perfect place for a romantic day of pampering in Iceland, and the therapeutic properties of the water make it a popular destination for those with skin diseases. The resort was opened to the public in 1987. Open year-round, with prices ranging from $50 for the basic package to $260 for the complete treatment, there are a range of packages to choose from.

**The endless sun:**

You can tell Iceland isn't going to be a beach vacation destination for couples just by looking at its name. But when the sun comes out in the summer, the sky are really breathtaking. During the months of May through August, visitors to Iceland may enjoy lengthy days bathed in what seems like an unending supply of sunshine.

A fantastic approach to see this extraordinary occurrence is to go to Þingvellir national park via one of the infamous F-roads in Iceland.

**Glacial hikes:**

Make sure you don't let yourself get too sunburned and miss out on one of Iceland's most stunning features: the graceful icy plains. You may go on guided glacier walks in Sólheimajökull or Svínafellsjökull, two glaciers situated on the island's southern coast.

Enjoy the glacial lagoons on a romantic boat cruise or paddle out into the wilderness as a couple to soak in the breathtaking scenery. Capture breathtaking images and create lasting memories of any of Iceland's frozen landscapes.

**Savor the Flavors of Icelandic Cuisine:**

If gourmet restaurants and local specialties are your idea of a romantic date, Iceland offers it everything. Reykjavik has a diverse selection of food and drink, including a growing vegan scene, and a romantic evening out at one of the city's fine dining establishments is easy to arrange. Indulge in the greatest Nordic cuisine made with the freshest local ingredients at the Michelin-starred Dill.

If ordering takeout and snuggling up with a movie is more your speed, then you should check out some of Reykjavik's fast food joints. Romantic doesn't have to mean pricey.

**Appreciate icelandic cuisine:**

Going on a romantic getaway to Iceland without taking pictures would be a huge regret. The stunning waterfalls of Iceland provide a once-in-a-lifetime picture opportunity that will capture the spirit of the place and its people for years to come. Among Iceland's waterfalls, Gullfoss is perhaps the most famous, but Seljalandsfoss is one of the most picturesque and romantic. The waterfall is encircled by a trail that leads you beyond the walls for an enchanting journey as you stroll in the mist.

On the other hand, Skógafoss is a great place to see a rainbow—or perhaps two—if you're in the mood for some enchanted color.

**Uncover local wildlife:**

Horseback riding is an exciting and novel way to explore the rugged topography of Iceland and take in the breathtaking scenery, making it an ideal vacation spot for nature enthusiasts.

If you're looking for an unforgettable experience, whale watching in Iceland is it. Húsavík, a village in northern Iceland, offers a fantastic view of whales throughout the summer.

**Soak at Reykjadur and other natural hot springs:**

When it comes to geothermal pools and hot springs in Iceland, it's not only the Blue Lagoon. If you and your partner are the daring kind, there are plenty of hidden sites to explore in search of a more obscure hot spring.

North of Reykjavík, at the Landbrotalaug Hot Pot, you may enjoy the water's warmth while taking in breathtaking views of the mountains, making it an ideal spot for a romantic getaway in Iceland.

Reykjadur is another fantastic place to go since it has a lovely 45-minute trek where you and your significant other can relax and take in the stunning scenery while being alone with nature.

**Take a stroll along the shore.**

Reykjavik is known for its delicious cuisine and picturesque coastlines, perfect for a romantic getaway. Indulge in a romantic walk down the shore and take in the breathtaking scenery, including passing boats, Videy island in the distance, and the majestic Mount Esja, which looms above the capital city both day and night.

Yoko Ono's outdoor memorial to John Lennon, the Imagine Peace Tower, can be seen in all its glory in December when it sends a beam of light into the sky.

**Reykjavík Church:**

An operational parish church with distinctive historical and architectural beauty, Hallgrímskirkja, towers above Reykjavik. Not only is it a free attraction, but it is also a popular spot for travelers.

Nevertheless, a thousand Icelandic Krona, or $7, will get you admission to the tower. Great for a romantic getaway, the tower is readily accessible thanks to its lift, and it offers breathtaking panoramic views of Reykjavik.

**Luxury accommodation:**

Throughout the nation of Iceland, you may find majestic luxury hotels and boutique escapes, in addition to the really unique experiences that the country is known for. Some that we really like are these:

A two-hour drive from Reykjavik lies Hótel Búðir, Hotel Ranga in Hella, Southern Iceland, and Hotel Borg in Reykjavik.

All of these hotels have breathtaking vistas that will put you and your loved one in the mood for romance, and if you're looking to up the ante on your vacation to Iceland, we have a variety of luxurious automobiles for hire.

Distribute the local ice cream "BragÔarefur":

What could be more romantic than sharing an ice cream cone with a significant other? Bragðarefur is the ideal place for anyone seeking to get involved in the local romance scene. Plus, bragðarefur isn't your average ice cream; it lets you customize your soft serve with a variety of toppings including fruit, sauce, and candy, making it a one-of-a-kind romantic treat.

# TRAVELING ON A BUDGET - MONEY SAVING TIPS

It is important to find ways to reduce costs without lowering the quality of your vacation. The good news is that there are a plethora of options for budget-friendly travel preparation and accommodation. Following these tips can help you save money without sacrificing the quality of your next trip.

**Ways to Reduce Travel Expenses**

So, what are some ways that tourists might save costs on their next vacation? For your next trip, here are 12 ways to save costs.

One simple approach to save costs on vacation is to prepare ahead of time by reading up on your location and its cuisine, traditions, and customs. The next step is to search for travel discounts and bargains that you can use, such as seasonal sales and promotional coupons. To keep to your budget, use a budgeting tool, such as a travel app, to monitor your spending.

**Plan Ahead:** When planning a vacation as a couple, it's best to get a head start so you can take advantage of discounts on airfare, lodging, and activities. Take a summer trip to Europe as an example; it's best to start searching for flights and accommodations in January or February. Because of this, you will have more time to look for the greatest discounts by comparing costs.

**Couple planning trip:** When planning a vacation as a couple, it's best to get a head start so you can take advantage of discounts on airfare, lodging, and activities. Take a summer trip to Europe as an example; it's best to start searching for flights and accommodations in January or February. Because of this, you will have more time to look for the greatest discounts by comparing costs.

**Be Flexible with Your Travel Dates:** If you can be flexible with when you go, you may save money on your trip. You may want to think about going during the off-season, when costs tend to be cheaper. Booking your vacation in closer proximity to your travel date may also help you take advantage of last-minute specials and discounts.

For a beach vacation, for instance, think about traveling in the spring or autumn, when it's still pleasant but there are less people. Or, to save money on hotels and flights, think about taking a city getaway during the week.

**Choose Budget-Friendly Accommodations:** Hotels may eat up a significant portion of a vacation budget, but there are methods to save costs without sacrificing quality. Hotels, especially budget hotels, are a good option since they are often less expensive than five-star hotels. Also, if you're going on a group trip, consider staying in a vacation rental, such as an Airbnb. You may earn free nights or savings by participating in a rewards program.

**Open a Travel-Friendly Bank Account:** It could be beneficial to create a bank account that allows you to travel more often if you do a lot of traveling. Among the perks include advantageous exchange rates, free ATM withdrawals overseas, and zero costs for foreign transactions. In addition, you may get travel insurance, airport lounge access, and cheap or even free international wire transfers offered by select institutions that are known to be travel-friendly.

You should compare the costs and benefits of several accounts offered by different banks before deciding on one to suit your specific travel demands. You may save costs and have more financial security when you create a bank account that is designed for travelers.

**Use Cashback or Rewards Cards:** Credit cards with cash back or incentives may be a great way to save money and get cool stuff. You may earn miles on flights, points at hotels, or even cash back on your travel purchases with many different credit card issuers. With these points, you may get a discount on your vacation or maybe even free lodging or airfare.

Pick a credit card whose perks complement your planned trips, and then use it wisely to keep from going into debt. Also, before you use your card overseas, check with your bank to see if there are any additional costs for international transactions. You may maximize your trip budget and receive great perks with a rewards card that you discover with little study.

**Eat Local Food:** You may save money and learn about the local culture by eating at eateries in your area. For a more genuine and affordable meal, choose a local restaurant instead than one that caters to tourists. In addition, dining at local establishments is a great way to meet locals and get insight into their culture.

**Utilize Free Attractions:** Museums, parks, and walking tours are just a few examples of the many free activities offered by cities and towns. You may view the sites and hear about the history of the area without breaking the bank by taking one of these. Free events and activities are often advertised in local publications and on the internet.

**Take Public Transportation:** One way to cut down on transportation expenses is to use public transit. Consider using the metro, bus, or train as an alternative to taxis. Another great way to get some exercise while seeing the city is to walk or hire a bike.

**Pack Light:** Reduce the amount of money you spend on baggage fees by packing lightly. Keep just the things you will absolutely need for your trip and leave the rest at home. Instead of spending money at the airport or on the airline, bring your own food and beverages to save money.

**Bring Your Own Snacks and Drinks:** The cost of eating out may quickly add up, so it's wise to carry your own snacks and beverages to keep costs down. For extended journeys or visits to nations with high food costs, this is a lifesaver. Be sure to bring along some refreshments in your carry-on or checked bag.

**Shop Around for Deals:** Look around for the greatest bargains on airfare, hotels, and activities. Finding the finest prices is made easy with the aid of several websites and applications. In order to be informed of exceptional deals, you can also register for email notifications from hotels and airlines.

**Use a Travel Agent:** If you want to discover the greatest prices on flights, hotels, and activities, a travel agent is your best bet. In addition, they may assist you in organizing your vacation and making sure everything runs well. For those who aren't sure where to begin, a travel agency is a wonderful resource. Now that you know how to save money on an adventure, you can plan your next trip with confidence and make wonderful memories without breaking the bank.

## CHAPTER NINE
### TOP 10 MUST-VISIT MUSEUMS IN ICELAND

The island of Iceland is home to a plethora of museums that will acquaint you with Icelandic culture and history via the telling of many fascinating tales. For those who prefer indoor activities or are history buffs, here is a blog post on the top museums in Iceland.

Even though there is a ton of options, I'll just give you my top ten. We all have different tastes, but no matter what you're into, you can find a museum—or museums—that cater to your interests! Some of the best things to do as a family with children of various ages are included here.

**The settlement exhibition:**

Step inside the Viking Age at this museum, which is also called Landnámssýningin in Icelandic. The main display hall of The Settlement Museum takes visitors on a journey back in time to the 930–1000 AD era, when the Vikings arrived in Iceland and resided here. Exhibited with several other artifacts are the painstakingly recreated remnants of the hall. All the details of Viking life are here for your perusal. Some interesting information about them, their territorial expansion, and their cultural impact, especially in Iceland, is accessible via touch displays. It also emphasizes the ways in which Icelandic nature has changed over the years.

Here in Reykjavík, near Aðalstraeti 10 & 16, you may find the Settlement Museum.
Available every day from 10:00 to 17:00
Adults must pay 27,40 ISK to enter. Kids under the age of 17, seniors (67 and over), and those with disabilities don't pay.

**The Icelandic National Museum:**

If you are interested in learning about the history of Icelandic life over the ages, you should visit this museum (Þjóðminjasafn Íslands). In this comprehensive resource, you will find information about this island nation's history, beliefs, religion, seafaring, agriculture, culture, costume, and trade links. Beautifully organized into sections with plenty of information, the exhibitions are a sight to see. Audio displays provide engaging narratives, while computers provide access to a plethora of supplementary information. At all times, you may find a photographic exhibition.

Located at Suðurgata 41, 101 Reykjavík, the National Museum of Iceland is open from 10:00 to 17:00 from Tuesday to Sunday.

Fees for entry:

Two thousand five hundred Icelandic crowns Seniors (67+) and students pay 1200 ISK, while children 0–17 and disabled people do not pay.

**Perlan:**

The glass-domed "The Pearl" is a remarkable example of contemporary architecture. It ranks well among Reykjavik's museums in terms of attendance. From there, you can take in breathtaking views of the city and its environs. The museum's inside is just as interesting as its exterior, however, with a variety of exhibits that shed light on the marvels of our planet. Among the many attractions here are a lava display, an indoor ice cave, and a planetarium dedicated to the Northern Lights.

Öskjuhlíð, 105 Reykjavík, Iceland is where you can find the Perlan Museum.

Any time between 9:00 and 22:00

Cost of admission: 5490 ISK for adults - Youths (ages 6–17) - A family ticket for two adults and two children costs 13,990 ISK (3290 ISK).

**Reykjavík maritime museum:**

Sjóminjasafnid, the museum, is really fantastic. To me, what stood out the most. Getting an Icelandic take on the "Cod Wars" was fascinating for a Brit like myself since it was so different from the UK's news coverage. Although the Icelanders' tactics weren't always ideal, I still believe they were correct. My interest in the fishing culture of Iceland was piqued since I grew up in close proximity to a large fishing town in the United Kingdom. Stories of courageous people who, despite facing adversity and tragedy, managed to find pleasure in life and remain strong. Additionally, a guided tour of the Coast Guard Vessel, Óðinn, is available at your convenience.

Grandagarður 8, 101 Reykjavík is the address of the Reykjavík Maritime Museum.

From 10:00 am until 7:00 pm every day

Entry fees: 2220 ISK for adults, 0–17 for children, 67 and up for seniors, and 3410 ISK for disabled people. Guided tours of the Óðinn and the museum cost 1710 and 3410 ISK, respectively.

**The saga museum:**

Visit the Sagas Museum if you are looking for an immersive experience with the Icelandic Sagas. Stunningly accurate sculptures of prominent and divisive figures from the Icelandic Sagas will transport you to the eras of ancient history's most momentous events. English, Icelandic, Russian, French, Spanish, and Swedish are the accessible audio guide languages.

If anybody would want to read it aloud or would like a hard copy, they may pick one up at reception.

Open daily from 10:00 to 17:00, the Saga Museum (Sögu Setrið) can be found at Grandagarður 2, 101 Reykjavík.

Fees for entry: Aged 3600 ISK Age group: 6–12 one thousand ISK Three thousand Icelandic crowns (ISK) for the student 3000 ISK for the disabled Aged 3000 ISK Pro

**Aurora reykjavík:**

The moment when the night sky is painted with nature's spectacular light display is unmatched. But when Mother Nature isn't cooperating, this is a fantastic backup plan! You will come away from this article with a solid grasp of the production of the northern lights thanks to the fascinating facts and breathtaking pictures. With our Northern Lights & Aurora Museum combination trip, you may even go on a personal quest for the northern lights after you've visited the museum.

Grandagarður 2, 101 Reykjavík is the address of Aurora Reykjavík.

Reopens at 1:00 every evening.

Adults must pay 2900 ISK to enter. Students pay 2500 ISK - Children (6-16) pay 1500 ISK

**The museum of phalalogy:**

Do you recall that I brought up questionable museum exhibits? Guess what? There isn't any other penis museum on the planet. There are almost two hundred penises on display, representing nearly every kind of terrestrial and marine animal found in Iceland. There is no other collection of this scale anywhere in the world.

Open everyday from 10:00 to 19:00, the Penis Museum can be found at Hafnartorg, Kalkofnsvegur 2, 101, Reykjavík.

Fees for entry: Individuals aged 13 and above pay 2750 ISK

**Árbær open air museum:** In this museum, you may see the lifestyles of Icelanders from very recent generations, even down to the great-great-grandparents of some of the current inhabitants. Carefully displayed here are actual homes from the time as well as commonplace household, agricultural, and fishing gear. The guided tours are well worth the admission price since the interpreters reenact historical events while dressed in period attire.

The location of Árbær Open Air Museum is 110 Reykjavík, at Kistuhylur 4

Hours of operation: 10:00 am to 7:00 pm (June through August) and 13:00 pm to 7:00 pm (September and May).

Fees for entry:

Costs 22,220 ISK for adults Student with a 1370 ISK student ID Kids (under the age of 17) don't pay; seniors (67 and above) and those with disabilities still don't pay.

**Viking Land**: You can find this museum near Keflavík, just on the coast. I think this is the best spot to start familiarizing yourself with Viking mythology the moment you arrive. There are three primary exhibits to be seen at this museum. An incredibly well-preserved model of the Viking ship Gokstad was found in Norway and is on display here. Additionally, you may see the

Smithsonian Institute's Vikings: The North Atlantic Saga exhibition, which delves into the topic of the Vikings' discovery of the Americas. The final exhibit provides evidence that clarifies the origins of the Icelandic colony.

Víkingabraut 1, 260 Reykjanesbær is where you may find Viking World.

From 10:00 am until 16:00 pm every day

Fees for entry: Total cost: 3,420 ISK for adults - Youth(7–16) A student would need 2160 ISK.

**Whales of iceland:** Located close to Reykjavik's city center, Whales of Iceland is renowned as Europe's biggest museum of its type. Listen to an audio commentary put together by experts including marine scientists and tour operators while you view 23 species of whales that appear just like the real thing. The museum welcomes visitors of all ages, making it an ideal outing for families. Dive with colossal creatures like sperm whales, blue whales, and North Atlantic right whales.

Located at Fiskislóð 23-25, 101 Reykjavík, the Whales of Iceland Museum is open everyday from 10:00 to 17:00.

Fees for entry: Adults Kids (0-6) go in free, while kids (7-15) pay 3900 ISK. 1950 Swedish crowns Two-person households with at least two children 7,800 Icelandic Krona

# CHAPTER TEN

## 7 DAYS IN ICELAND: AN ITINERARY FOR FIRST-TIME TRAVELERS

The sights you want to visit in Iceland will dictate your itinerary. Hikers of all skill levels will find an abundance of trails in Iceland to suit their needs. Iceland is a photographer's paradise, with many breathtaking locations waiting to be discovered.

**Day 1 – The Golden Circle, Some Breathtaking Waterfalls and an Iconic Planewreck**
We rented a hotel near the airport the night before our late-night flight from Germany to Iceland, and we promptly slept off upon arrival. That gave us the opportunity to begin our Iceland itinerary over, with the whole day at our disposal. Before setting off on our ideal road trip around Iceland, we did something that should be on every visitor's list.

**Golden Circle:**
Many of Iceland's most well-known attractions make up what is known as the Golden Circle. All of them are in close proximity to one another, making it an ideal spot for first-time visitors to get

a feel for the breathtaking nature of Iceland. Thingvellir National Park, Kerid, Gullfoss Waterfall, and the Geysir Geothermal Area make up the Golden Circle. You can visit the whole Golden Circle in a day, but you may certainly spend more time there if you so choose.

**Skógafoss:**

The Skógafoss is the Icelandic waterfall that I have seen most often in my time spent on social media. And the top spot is rightfully its! It is quite stunning, particularly when the Lupines are in bloom. Arrive later in the day to escape the throng if you want to snap photographs here.

**Solheimasandur Plane Wreck:**

The southern region of Iceland is jam-packed with some of Iceland's most picturesque locations! Tourists and photographers alike congregate to the Solheimasandur Plane Wreck. Getting there is an exciting journey in and of itself. Going alone isn't for the faint of heart, so arm yourself with knowledge before you go off. The trip will be worthwhile in the end!

**Your Stay for the Night: Hótel Dyrhólaey:**

Cuddling up is in order after a day of exciting Icelandic excursions! In addition to a pleasant restaurant, the rooms of Hótel Dyrhólaey are warm and inviting.

**Day 2 – Black Sand Beach Reynisfjara, Vík í Mýrdal, Fjaðrárgljúfur, Jökulsárlón, Diamond Beach:**

Everyone who knows me well knows that I really like breakfast buffets, and because we stayed at Hótel Dyrhólaey, they provided one for us. Coffee, orange juice, and delicious herring were the perfect way to start the day. It was then time to go sightseeing in Iceland!

**Black Sand Beach Reynisfjara | 10-minute drive from the Hotel:**

Our day begins with a visit to Reynisfjara Beach! I must issue a warning before I extol the untamed beauty of this beach and its untamed rock formations. Be warned that Reynisfjara Beach is among the most perilous in all of Iceland when you plan your vacation there. The issue is that the waves are quite powerful, so once they swallow you whole, there's no turning back. That is why, for your own safety, you should maintain a minimum distance from the shoreline.

Reynisfjara Beach is among the most breathtaking locations you will ever see, dangers be damned. The combination of the dark sand and the basalt pillars creates a stunning backdrop. When the puffins are in season, you may see them soaring about and building their nests if you look carefully enough. Sunset is the most picturesque time of day for it as well!

**Vík í Mýrdal | 10-minute drive:**
Come to Vík for a quick pit break if you're running low on petrol or food. It has a beautiful church and all the necessary supplies for the following several days' preparations. I am referring about food and souvenirs from Iceland! All of your favorite Icelandic woollen goods, including sweaters, mittens, and caps, are available here. Lava salt and Viking jewelry are also part of the package. During the trip, I adored reading the Icelandic fairy stories that I brought home in a book.

Once you depart from the town, continue along the main road for a while. In the summer, the fields next to this road are transformed into a verdant paradise by the lupines that border it. Due to its breathtaking beauty, it is an ideal spot to pause for some photographs.

**Fjaðrárgljúfur | 50-minute drive:**
The day's itinerary continues with a visit to a viewpoint. What a perspective! In the canyon known as Fjaðrárgljúfur, a little stream dug its way through the mountain over an extensive period of time. This site may finally be appreciated. In addition, I like it because, after a long day of traveling, it was refreshing to be able to walk a little to the top perspectives.
Just so you know, I may be very obnoxious, but please hear me out. Sitting for that one perfect Instagram image is a popular pastime. But a barrier has made this area even less safe. Climbing the fence to acquire the photo is still done by some. No shot, no matter how great you think it is, is worth endangering your safety for. Have a safe trip!

**Jökulsárlón | 1 hour and 45-minute drive:**

We are now heading to our final two destinations of the day, both of which are quite remarkable, after Fjaðrárgljúfur. Glacier debris falls into the bay of Jökulsárlón. Afterwards, the glaciers are carried out of the bay into the ocean by the prevailing current. Those interested in getting a better view may book boat cruises to get up close to the glaciers' pieces. Observing these azure marvels from a safe distance, we remained still. We were able to see a pod of seals lounging around as we were there. I really like locations like Iceland for that same reason. Even from a distance, you may observe nature, and you can view these stunning creatures in their natural habitat!

**Diamond Beach | 10-minute walk:**

You may also locate the one site you spotted on Instagram earlier, almost right near to Jökulsárlón. Parts of the boulders washed up from Jökulsárlón end up on Diamond Beach, a black beach. When you search for them on social media, the beach appears just beautiful, and these things seem just like diamonds. Nevertheless, I was quite let down. Perhaps my prior experience on the beach had inflated my expectations, but I failed to see it. I didn't think the ice looked very attractive since it was so little.

**Time to rest: Dining & Sleeping in Höfn | 1 hour drive:**

We were anticipating a hot supper and a comfortable bed after a hard day of traveling. There are two of these in Höfn! An excellent spot to stop at this stage of your road journey is Höfn, a little town in southern Iceland that lies right on the water. It offers some great lodging options and some fantastic eateries. Something simple but endearing was our choice. Höfn Cottages has a charming little cottage that was just right for the two of us as we spent the night on the road. We enjoyed the most amazing Icelandic lamb for our meal at the Pakkhus after we settled in.

**Day 3 – Sea Viewpoint, Skútafoss, Nykurhylsfoss, Klifbrekku Waterfall, Haifoss, Seydisfjordur:**

You will awaken in Höfn on the third day of this adventure and set off to hunt the most amazing waterfalls. Your next stop will be a picturesque beach hamlet for an early supper! And after a relaxing soak in the hot tub, you can drift off to sleep with the sound of a few horses as your only companions!

**Sea Viewpoint | 12-minute drive:**

Coffee with a view is one of my favorite things to do. Our most wonderful one was with us this morning for ours. The perfect place to get some coffee and breakfast is only eight minutes away from Höfn, at a seaside viewpoint.

**Skútafoss | 12-minute drive:**

Whenever we go on road trips, I'm happy to get out of the car and wander about a little. Taking a short stroll to Skútafoss, a little waterfall near the Sea Viewpoint, allowed us to take the opportunity. Skútafoss may not be the most spectacular waterfall on this route, but it is a good reminder of what you will encounter. The takeaway here is that you should never miss an opportunity to go off the usual path, and Iceland is no exception. Iceland is full with little treasures that deserve your undivided attention.

**Nykurhylsfoss | 1 hour and 20-minute drive:**

The third day of your Iceland trip is when you'll see the waterfall, I swear! The next waterfall is waiting for you at the end of a drive through the most spectacular fjords you can imagine! Bring some guts since the slope you'll have to drive up to get to the parking lot is rather steep. However, the sheer force of the waterfall is what really stands out. The noise level is so high that you almost can't carry on a conversation while in its vicinity. The water here isn't just falling; it's pouring, so make sure to pack your finest raincoat.

**Klifbrekku Waterfall | 2-hour drive:**

One of the most picturesque drives of your life awaits you as you go from Nykurhylsfoss to the next waterfall. Leaving it off of this Iceland itinerary would be a huge letdown. But for the time being, all there is to it is the drive in between two stunning waterfalls. One of the most underappreciated waterfalls in Iceland, Klifbrekku, is also one of my favorites. We made it there safely, albeit we were a little worried about the experience of driving there in the cheapest automobile available.

**Haífoss & Gufufoss | 55-minute drive:**

While going across Iceland, you will pass two more must-see waterfalls on your route to lunch. And easy to use, even if you're not very brave while you're at the wheel of the stirrup!

### Seydisfjordur | 5-minute drive:

There are a few hotels and a grocery in the charming small fishing hamlet, so it's not only a good area to have lunch or early supper, but also a good spot to spend the night. We enjoyed the rainbow road and strolled around the few streets for just a little bit. At last, we stopped for lunch at El Grillo Bar. After that, we went grocery shopping for a quick supper at our hotel.

### Cosy Cottage-Álfabakki-with hot tub | 50-minute drive:

The smartest option we made was to travel a little farther and reserve the Cosy Cottage in Álfabakki with a hot tub so that we could begin our journey the following day closer to all the sites. The only other creatures we saw were a herd of amiable horses, one of which was carrying a baby. We cuddled up and watched Netflix for the remainder of the evening, enjoying the sound of waterfalls as we drifted off to sleep.

### Day 4 – Hochebene, Dettifoss, Myvatn, Goðafoss, Dinner in Húsavík im Naustið:

One of the highlight days of your schedule is about to arrive! As you drive up to a bizarre location that makes you think of the moon or Mars, you'll see Europe's tallest waterfall, see volcanic eruptions up close, and end the day with supper in the most inviting spot you can think of!

### Driving Route 1 | 1 hour 45-minute drive:

The day begins with a visit to a waterfall—just what you'd expect in Iceland—but getting there is quite the adventure! Once you begin to drive uphill, the scenery will change dramatically with every meter you go higher. Beyond spectacular now, it's going to take on a surreal quality. There is a complete lack of plant life, and upon awakening, we found ourselves engulfed in a haze. Almost otherworldly, it seemed like a dream.

### Dettifoss:

You will eventually reach your next destination, the formidable Dettifoss, albeit the scenery doesn't alter much until then. This is the most impressive waterfall in all of Europe, and it will wow you. Since the waterfall is a common stop for tour busses, there is also a pleasant public restroom here in case you are concerned. It was a relief for me. We lingered at the base of Dettifoss for some time, taking it all in. Just remember to remain on the pleasant routes that have been laid out for you.

**Hverir & Myvatn | 35-minute drive:**
Your next stop will be just as surreal as your journey there. Famous for its bubbling hot springs, Hverir is a geothermal site. You should probably not go too near to it while you're here because it's so hot—I mean, boiling hot. The region as a whole serves to highlight the fact that Iceland is continually being formed and transformed by its volcanic activity. Hverir and Myvatn are the places where you may experience this for yourself. And if you go too near to the vapor from the pools at Hverir, you'll also smell it.

Even though it's only a short drive from Hverir, Myvatn is well worth spending some time here. The verdant scenery was breathtaking, and it was fascinating to see the wide range of effects caused by volcanic eruptions. Just a short distance from the seemingly lifeless landscape of Hverir is a paradisiacal destination like Myvatn, complete with hot water. This is where we went for our second lengthy stroll; it was very beautiful and something you shouldn't miss!

**Goðafoss | 35-minute drive:**
Waterfalls often fascinate me, but I really liked this one. Goðafoss can be seen from both above and below, which is a wonderful shift of viewpoint. I really adore the waterfall itself. And if you haven't gotten some Icelandic presents for your loved ones yet, you're missing out! The gift store just next to the waterfall has an incredible assortment! One of my favorite pasta seasonings is black lava salt, which is my favorite ingredient overall.

**Accommodation & and dinner in Húsavík at the Naustið | 40-minute drive:**
I thought it was quite a lengthy day. Snuggling down with a warm meal after all that travel was a welcome relief. The Guesthouse Hagi was our overnight destination, and it was among my

favorite parts of that trip. Staying in this little cottage adjacent to a little river is sure to put you at rest. I was tempted to perform some light yoga on the front porch, and I was looking forward to starting my day with a cup of coffee in this same spot. But there were still some hungry tummies that needed to be filled before we could go slumber. Our meal was served in the Naustið, a charming seafood restaurant in Húsavík. We were left wanting more ocean adventures after trying everything there (hint for tomorrow's activities!) since it was all so amazing.

**Day 5 – Puffin & Whale Watching Tour, Scenic Drive:**
I'm really excited for today! We finally went whale viewing in Húsavík, an event we had been waiting for, so we brought our warmest clothing and medication for motion sickness. This is apart from the fact that what lies ahead is one of the most picturesque drives you will ever experience!

**Puffin & Whale Watching Tour:**
Iceland is a fantastic spot to see whales up close, despite the country's less-than-stellar past with these majestic animals. Seeing whales in Iceland during the summer is almost assured, whether from a boat or the beach (we saw more later in the day!). In fact, going on a whale-watching excursion may be the most memorable part of your vacation!

We chose a two-part itinerary: first, a short drive to an islet that, in the summer, is home to a massive puffin colony! We are really thrilled to see these adorable, plump guys in their own environment since we are head over heels with them.

Once you have spent some time watching the puffins, you will be led back into the Húsavík fjord. You and the team will be out on the ocean looking for whales. Sometimes, when they're feeling frisky, you may even see them hunting and leaping out of the water. Unfortunately, most of the whales fled the fjord the day before our trip due to a storm, so we were a little unfortunate. Anyway, it was more than compensated for by witnessing even a single whale up close!

**Scenic Drive | 4h 10 minutes:**

We got back in our vehicle and hit the road as soon as we were on firm ground again! According to Google Maps, the distance between our current location and our new flat in Blönduós is really very short. But I highly suggest you follow our lead and take the longer, more picturesque path. One of the most underappreciated aspects of Iceland is the driving around the stunning cliffs and landscapes. In this case, I would suggest picking up some cinnamon buns from the Húsavík bakery and then making a pit stop in Héðinsfjörður for a quick bite in the afternoon. There has never been a cinnamon bun with a more picturesque setting!

**Blönduós & Harbour Restaurant & Bar:**

We checked into our accommodation for the night after we got in the village of Blönduós. We found just what we were searching for at the Kiljan Apartment—a clean, pleasant, and reasonably priced location to spend the night. We had a fantastic meal at the Harbour Restaurant, which is a short drive away, for our evening. We were both exhausted from the anti-motion sickness medication, so we went to bed afterwards.

**Day 6: Hvitserkur, Kolugljú, Gerdberg Cliffs, Kirkjufellsfoss & the best sushi in Iceland:**

The following is just as spectacular, with stunning ocean vistas and maybe even a few of picturesque waterfalls.

By the day's conclusion, you'll have eaten all the finest Icelandic cuisine and be sleeping soundly in a comfortable accommodation on the island's eastern coast.

**Hvitserkur | 1 hour drive:**

The day begins with a visit to a world-renown rock formation! Here people debate whether this rock looks more like an elephant, a rhinoceros, or a dinosaur; ultimately, it's up to you to make up your mind. However, a dinosaur would be my choice. The rock is certainly worth a visit, but the stunning view of the water and beach is what really sold me.

**Kolugljúfur Canyon | 40-minute drive:**

A breathtaking canyon with a beautiful waterfall! On your journey to the eastern side of Iceland, be sure to stop in Kolugljúfur Canyon for some refreshments, some scenery, and some climbing activity.

**Gerðuberg Cliffs | 2-hour drive:**
I am always astounded by basalt pillars. Plan a stop at the Gerðuberg Cliffs if you want to view some very stunning ones; there's simply something about them. We were astounded by them as we strolled past them.

**Kirkjufellsfoss | 50-minute:**
Is this point at the final waterfall sufficient to warrant your attention? This is the last waterfall in Iceland, but don't be downhearted; there is much more to see and do in this beautiful country. Although it isn't as massive as some of the others on my Iceland itinerary, I adored it nonetheless for the breathtaking landscapes that surrounded it.

**Gamla Riff & Viðvík Restaurant:**
Checking into the hotel for the night is already in the cards after Kirkjufellsfoss. Gamla Rif is a breathtakingly beautiful inn with rooms that beg you to sink into a warm embrace. The public bathroom was spotless, so we didn't mind using it at all. Like the days before, we stopped by for a brief pit break on our way to get supper, and I must say, we discovered an incredible spot! An exceptional meal is served at the charming and fashionable Viðvík. I was really taken aback by the grilled salad that we had as an appetizer. The main course was what I describe as "the best sushi in Iceland," and to this day, I can't help but fantasize about it.

**Day 7: Drive to Reykjavík & Snorkeling in Silfra:**
We still had a lot of traveling to accomplish on this final full day of our plan, but you may fill this journey by stopping at less frequented routes if you want to. If you're bored with climbing and chasing waterfalls all day, you may alternatively spend the first part of the day exploring Reykjavík! Even though we would have missed out on seeing Iceland's capital, we went with option one. Whatever the case may be, the most spectacular experience will take place in the afternoon of Day 7.

**Snorkeling in the Silfra Fissure | 1-hour drive:**

If you were to imagine crystal pure water, the first image that would likely pop into your head would be a tropical island with a school of tiny, brightly colored fish swimming about you. Iceland, however, is home to some of the world's purest waters. The water entering the Silfra Fissure is very pure because it passes through a series of sedimentary strata that act as a filter. Plus, you get to see it for yourself!

Our only instruction on the day of our expedition was to come prepared, with dry, warm clothes and a spare pair of clothes. Put on your dry suit—a workout in and of itself—to begin your snorkeling adventure. Assuming it lives up to its claims, this suit should keep water at bay. Because the water is so chilly, that is rather cozy. Even while it's okay, I did notice that the majority of the suits leaked somewhat. Putting on the suit allows you to practice your most penguin-like gait before diving into the water.

You can see far and deep into the lake, and the purity is really stunning. A little stream carries you downstream, leaving you with no choice except to float leisurely through the rift until you can find a way out. Plus, you won't even need to know how to swim—the suit will have you floating effortlessly like a cork.
The charming Motel Arctic Wind will be your home for the night. It's conveniently located near your next and last stop on your journey, so the drive will be worthwhile in the evening.

**Day 8: Unwinding in the Blue Lagoon & Heading Home:**

The Blue Lagoon is located at the very end of this tour. It is one of my fondest recollections of our road trip to Iceland since it was the most luxurious spa treatment I have ever had. There, geothermal extraction wells provide a pale blue water for your bath. The algae that give the water its pale blue hue also happen to be very beneficial to your health. You get these fantastic face masks made of lagoon mud and beverages with any of the three experience packages that you may pick from when you book. The Blue Lagoon was the ideal place to complete our seven-day road trip and relax. It was fantastic, and we remained for four hours before leaving for the airport.

Made in the USA
Monee, IL
03 August 2024

63227325R10129

ISBN 9798877303386